# love

## A Guide *for* Prayer

# love

# A Guide *for* Prayer

Jacqueline Syrup Bergan *and* Sister Marie Schwan

LOYOLA PRESS.
A JESUIT MINISTRY
Chicago

## LOYOLA PRESS.
### A JESUIT MINISTRY

3441 N. Ashland Avenue
Chicago, Illinois 60657
(800) 621-1008
www.loyolapress.com

The first edition of this book was published by Saint Mary's Press, (Winona MI: 1985). A revised and updated edition was published by The Word Among Press (Ijamsville, MD: 2004).

*Cover images, top: iStockphoto/pederk; bottom: Thinkstock/iStockphoto*

**Library of Congress Cataloging-in-Publication Data**
Bergan, Jacqueline Syrup.
  Love : a guide for prayer / Jacqueline Syrup Bergan, Marie Schwan.
    p. cm. -- (Take and receive series)
  Originally published: Rev. and updated ed. Ijamsville, Md. : Word Among Us Press, 2004. (Take and receive series).
  Includes bibliographical references (p.        ) and index.
  ISBN-13: 978-0-8294-3611-2
  ISBN-10: 0-8294-3611-1
  1. Spiritual exercises. 2. Bible--Meditations. 3. Catholic Church--Prayers and devotions.  I. Schwan, Marie. II. Title.
    BX2182.3.B47 2011
    248.3'2088282--dc23

                                                             2011028459

Printed in United States of America
19 20 21 22 23 24 25 26 27 28  Versa  12 11 10 9 8 7 6 5 4 3

To Leonard
—Jackie

To my sisters
—Marie

Lord my God,
when Your love spilled over into creation
You thought of me.

I am
from love
of love
for love.

Let my heart, O God, always
    recognize,
    cherish,
    and enjoy your goodness in all of creation.

Direct all that is me toward your praise;
Teach me reverence for every person, all things.
Energize me in your service.

Lord God,
May nothing ever distract me from your love . . .
Neither health nor sickness
    wealth nor poverty
    honor nor dishonor
    long life nor short life.

May I never seek nor choose to be other
    than You intend or wish.
Amen.

# Contents

## Part Three—God's Creation

## Part Four—Spiritual Freedom

# Part Five—Commitment

# Introduction

TWENTY-FIVE YEARS AGO, WE WERE together in ministry on the plains of northwestern Minnesota, bringing to parishes days and evenings of prayer. There we witnessed, and were touched by, the goodness, openness, and spiritual hunger of those who came to learn to pray and to spend time in prayer. We felt compelled to provide a follow-up to these brief spiritual experiences; thus was born the dream of writing a self-help approach to the Spiritual Exercises of St. Ignatius of Loyola. Our own experience of the gift and power of Ignatian Spirituality created a desire to share its richness.

What we experienced as a call became a somewhat wild and faith-filled commitment to provide, at a time when such was not widely available, an approach to the Spiritual Exercises, making this Christocentric dynamic of conversion available for people who did not have the luxury of local retreat centers nor spiritual directors—some were living in parishes without resident pastors. We were so convinced of the importance of this project that we agreed that even if we were unable to find a publisher willing to take a risk with a series written by two unknown women from Minnesota, we would complete the series and wait for its moment.

We experienced the blessing of God when Bishop Victor Balke gave us a loan of $7000 to have the first volume printed. We sold 2000 copies—to all our family and friends—and paid our debt. We still had 3,000 copies on hand. Then a publisher approached us, and the series was on its way. It was always more God's work than ours.

It is with delight and gratitude that we witness the new edition of *Love*, the first volume of the Take and Receive series. We are happy that the series is finding a home at Loyola Press, which has as its mission to be a repository of Ignatian spirituality.

Through the past twenty-five years the series has supported the prayer life of men and women, lay and religious. It has provided a basis for spiritual direction, been used as a text in some college courses, and has served as a guide for prayer groups—and continues to do so.

The content of this new edition remains remarkably unchanged. It speaks, we think, of the enduring quality of the series.

Over the years we have kept in prayer all those who have made use of these books, and all who supported us in the writing and the publishing of them. Our prayer for each one has been, and continues to be, the prayer of St. Paul:

"I pray that the God of our Lord Jesus Christ, the Father of glory, may give you a spirit of wisdom and revelation as you come to know him, so that, with the eyes of your heart enlightened, you may know what is the hope to which he has called you, what are the riches of his glorious inheritance among the saints, and what is the immeasurable greatness of his power for us who believe, according to the working of his great power" (Ephesians 1:17–19).

Jacqueline Syrup Bergan    Marie Schwan, CSJ

Feast of the Transfiguration, 2011

# Getting Started: How to Pray

*Lord, teach us to pray.*

LUKE 11:1

PRAYER IS OUR PERSONAL RESPONSE to God's presence. Just as Jesus was present to his first disciples, so God is present to each of us every day. Therefore, we can approach him reverently with a listening heart. He speaks first to us. In prayer, we acknowledge his presence and in gratitude respond to him in love. The focus is always on God and what he does. The following suggestions are offered as ways that will help us be attentive to God's word and to respond to it uniquely.

## Daily Pattern of Prayer

For each period of prayer, use the following pattern:

### Before Prayer—Preparation

Plan to spend at least twenty minutes to one hour in prayer daily. Although there is nothing "sacred" about sixty minutes, most people find that an hour better provides for quieting themselves and entering fully into the Scripture passage. To better prepare your heart and mind, take time the evening before to read the commentary as well as the Scripture passage for the following day. Just before falling asleep, recall the Scripture passage.

## During Prayer—Structuring Your Time

As you begin your prayer time, quiet yourself; be still inside and out. Relax and breathe in and out, deeply and slowly. Repeat several times.

Realize that you are nothing without God and declare your dependence on him. Ask him for the grace you want and need. Then read and reflect on your chosen Scripture passage, using the appropriate form, such as meditation for poetic and nonstory passages or contemplation for stories or events. (See the section on the variety of ways to pray privately, page 3). Close the prayer period with a time of conversation with Jesus and his Father. Speak to God personally and listen attentively. Conclude with the Our Father.

## After Prayer—Review

At the conclusion of the prayer period, take the time for review and reflection. The purpose of the review is to heighten your awareness of how God has been present to you during the prayer period. The review focuses primarily on what St. Ignatius described as the interior movements of consolation and desolation as they are revealed in your feelings of joy, peace, sadness, fear, ambivalence, anger, or any other emotion.

Often it is in the review that we become aware of how God has responded to our request for a particular grace or of what he may have said to us. Writing the review provides for personal accountability, and it is a precious record of our spiritual journey. To write the review is a step toward knowing ourselves as God sees us.

In the absence of a spiritual director or spiritual companion, the writing helps fill the need for evaluation and clarification. If you have a spiritual director, the written review offers an excellent means of preparing to share your prayer experience.

Keep a notebook or journal with you during prayer. After each prayer period, indicate the date and the Scripture passage that was the subject of your reflection. Then answer each of the following questions: Was there any word or phrase that particularly struck you? How did you feel? Were you peaceful? Loving? Trusting? Sad? Discouraged? What do these feelings say to you? How are you more aware of God's presence? Is there some point to which you should return during your next prayer period?

# A Variety of Ways to Pray Privately

There are various forms of scriptural prayer. Different forms appeal to different people. Eventually, by trying various methods, we become adept at using approaches that are appropriate to particular passages and are in harmony with our personality and needs. This guide will make use of seven forms.

## 1. Meditation

In meditation, one approaches the Scripture passage as though it were a love letter. This approach is especially helpful in praying poetic passages.

To use this method, read the passage slowly, aloud or in a whisper, savoring the words and letting them wash over you. Stay with the words that especially catch your attention; absorb them the way the thirsty earth receives the rain. Keep repeating a word or phrase, aware of the feelings that are awakened in you as well as a sense of God's presence.

Read and reread the passage lovingly, as you would a letter from a dear friend, or as you would softly sing the chorus of a song.

## 2. Contemplation

In contemplation, we enter a life event or story passage of Scripture. We enter the passage by way of imagination, making use of all our senses. Theologians tell us that through contemplation we are able to "recall and be present at the mysteries of Christ's life" (13, p. 149).* The Spirit of Jesus, present within us through baptism, teaches us just as Jesus taught the apostles. The Spirit recalls and enlivens the particular mystery into which we enter through prayer. As in the Eucharist, the risen Jesus makes present the paschal mystery, in contemplation he brings forth the particular event we are contemplating and presents himself within that mystery. God allows us to imagine ourselves present in a specific Scripture passage, where we can encounter Jesus face-to-face.

To use this method, enter the story as if you were there. Watch what happens; listen to what is being said. Become part of the story, assuming the role of one of the persons. Then look at each of the individuals. What does he or she experience? To whom does each one speak? Ask yourself, "What difference does it make for my life, my family, for society, if I hear the message?"

---

* Numbers are keyed to the Bibliography, pp. 139–142

In the Gospel stories, be sure to talk with Jesus. *Be there* with him and for him. *Want him*; *hunger* for him. *Listen* to him. *Let him* be for you what he wants to be. *Respond to him.*

## 3. Centering Prayer

The Cistercian monk and writer M. Basil Pennington has noted, "In centering prayer we go beyond thought and image, beyond the senses and the rational mind to that center of our being where God is working a wonderful work" (25, p. 18).

Centering prayer is a very simple, pure form of prayer, frequently without words. It is a path toward contemplative prayer, an opening of our hearts to the Spirit dwelling within us. In centering prayer, we travel down into the deepest center of ourselves. It is the point of stillness within us where we most experience being created by a loving God who is breathing us into life.

To enter centering prayer requires that we recognize our dependence on God and surrender to his Spirit of love. *"Likewise the Spirit helps us in our weakness . . . that very Spirit intercedes with sighs too deep for words"* (Romans 8:26). The Spirit of Jesus within us cries out, *"Abba! Father!"* (Romans 8:15).

To use this method, sit quietly, comfortable and relaxed. Rest within your longing and desire for God. Move to the center within your deepest self. This movement can be facilitated by imagining yourself slowly descending in an elevator, walking down flights of stairs, descending a mountain, or going down into a deep pool of water.

In the stillness, become aware of God's presence. *"Be still, and know that I am God!"* (Psalm 46:10). Peacefully absorb his love.

# 4. Prayer Word

One means of centering prayer is the use of a prayer word. It can be a single word or a phrase. It can be a word from Scripture or one that arises spontaneously from within your heart. The word or phrase represents, for you, the fullness of God. Variations of the prayer word may include the name "Jesus" or what is known as the Jesus Prayer: "Lord, Jesus Christ, Son of God, have mercy on me, a sinner."

To use this method, repeat the word or phrase slowly to yourself in harmony with your breathing. For example, say the first part of the Jesus Prayer while inhaling, the second half while exhaling.

# 5. Meditative Reading

.....................................................................................

*So I opened my mouth, and he gave me the scroll to eat. He said . . . eat this scroll that I give you and fill your stomach with it. Then I ate it; and in my mouth it was as sweet as honey.*

EZEKIEL 3:2–3

.....................................................................................

One of the approaches to prayer is reflective reading of Scripture or other spiritual writings. Spiritual reading is always enriching to our life of prayer, but it is especially helpful in times when prayer is difficult or dry.

To use this method, read slowly, pausing periodically to allow the words and phrases to settle inside you. When a thought resonates deeply, stay with it, allowing the fullness of it to penetrate your being. Relish the word received. Respond authentically and spontaneously, as in a dialogue.

# 6. Journaling

*The mystery was made known to me . . . as I wrote, . . . a reading of which will enable you to perceive my understanding of the mystery of Christ.*

EPHESIANS 3:3–4

Journaling is meditative writing. When we place pen on paper, spirit and body cooperate to release our true selves. There is a difference between journaling and keeping a journal. To journal is to experience God's presence as we see ourselves in a new light and as fresh images rise to the surface from deep within. Journaling requires putting aside preconceived ideas and control.

Meditative writing is like writing a letter to one we love. We recall memories, clarify our convictions, and allow affections to well up within us. In writing, we may discover that emotions are intensified and prolonged.

Because of this, journaling can also serve in identifying and healing hidden feelings such as anger, fear, and resentment. When we write to God honestly, he can begin to heal past hurts or memories that have stayed with us for years. In addition, journaling can give us a deeper appreciation for the written word as we encounter it in Scripture.

Journaling in prayer can take various forms:

- Write a letter addressed to God.

- Write a conversation between yourself and someone else. The other person may be Jesus or another significant person; the dialogue can also be about an event, an experience, or a value. For example, you can give death, separation, or wisdom personal attributes and imagine each as a person with whom you can converse.

- Write an answer to a question, such as, *"What do you want me to do for you?"* (Mark 10:51) or *"Why are you weeping?"* (John 20:15).

- Allow Jesus or another person in Scripture to "speak" to you through the pen.

# 7. Repetition

......................................................................................

*I will remain quietly meditating upon the point in which I have found what I desire without any eagerness to go on till I have been satisfied.*

St. Ignatius of Loyola (31, p. 110)

......................................................................................

Repetition is the return to a previous period of prayer for the purpose of allowing the movements of God to deepen within the heart. Through repetitions, we fine-tune our sensitivities to God and to how he speaks in our prayer and in our life circumstances. The prayer of repetition teaches us to understand who we are in light of how God sees us and who God is revealing himself to be for us.

Repetition is a way of honoring God's word to us in the earlier prayer period. It is recalling and pondering an earlier conversation with one we love. It is as if we say to God, "Tell me that again; what did I hear you saying?" In this follow-up conversation or repetition, we open ourselves to a healing presence that often transforms whatever sadness and confusion we may have experienced the first time we prayed.

In repetitions, not only does the consolation (joy, warmth, peace) deepen, but the desolation (pain, sadness, confusion) frequently moves to a new level of understanding and acceptance within God's plan for us.

To use this method, select a period of prayer to repeat in which you have experienced a significant movement of joy, sadness, or confusion. You might also select a period in which nothing seemed to happen—perhaps because of your lack of readiness at the time.

To begin, recall the feelings of the first period of prayer. Use as a point of entry the scene, word, or feeling that was previously most significant. Allow the Spirit to direct the inner movements of your heart during this time of prayer.

# Four Spiritual Practices and Helps

## 1. Examen of Consciousness

*O LORD, you have searched me and known me.*

PSALM 139:1

The examen of consciousness is the instrument by which we discover how God has been present to us and how we have responded to his presence through the day. St. Ignatius believed this practice was so important that, in the event it was impossible to have a formal prayer period, it would sustain one's vital link with God.

The examen of consciousness is not to be confused with an examination of conscience in which penitents are concerned with their failures. It is, rather, an exploration of how God is present within the events, circumstances, and feelings of our daily lives. What the review is to the prayer period, the examen is to our daily life. The daily discipline of an authentic practice of the examen brings about a balance that is essential for growth in relationship to God, to self, and to others. The method reflects the "dynamic movement of personal love: what we always want to say to a person whom we truly love in the order in which we want to say it. . . . Thank you . . . Help me . . . I love you . . . I'm sorry . . . Be with me" (10, pp. 34–35).

The following prayer is a suggested approach to the examen. The written response can be incorporated into the prayer journal:

- God, my Father, I am totally dependent on you. Everything is a gift from you. *All is gift.* I give you thanks and praise for the gifts of this day.

- Lord, I believe you work through and in time to reveal me to myself. Please give me an increased awareness of how you are guiding and shaping my life, as well as a more sensitive awareness of the obstacles I put in your way.

- You have been present in my life today. Be near, now, as I reflect on

    —your presence in the *events* of today

    —your presence in the *feelings* I experienced today

    —your *call* to me

    —my *response* to you

- Father, I ask your loving forgiveness and healing. The particular event of this day that I most want healed is . . .

- Filled with hope and a firm belief in your love and power, I entrust myself to your care and strongly affirm . . . (Claim the gift you most desire, most need; believe that God desires to give you that gift.)

## 2. Faith Sharing

*For where two or three are gathered in my name, I am there among them.*

MATTHEW 18:20

In the creation of community, it is essential that members communicate intimately with one another about the core issues of their lives. For the Christian, this is faith sharing, and it is an extension of daily solitary prayer.

A faith-sharing group, whether part of a parish, lay movement, or diocesan program, is not a discussion group, sensitivity session, or social gathering. Members do not come together to share and receive intellectual or theological insights. Nor is the purpose of faith sharing the accomplishment of some predetermined task. Instead, the purpose is to listen and to be open to God as he continues to reveal himself in the church community represented in the small group that comes together in his name. The fruit of faith sharing is the "building up" of the church, the body of Christ (Ephesians 4:12).

The approach of faith sharing is one of reading and reflecting together on the word of God. Faith sharing calls us to share with one another, from deep within our hearts, what it means to be a follower of Christ in our world today. To enter faith sharing authentically is to know and love one another in Christ, whose Spirit is the bonding force of community.

An image that faith-sharing groups may find helpful is that of a pool into which pebbles are dropped. The group gathers in a circle around a pool. Like a pebble being gently dropped into the water, each one offers a reflection—his or her "word" from God. In the shared silence, each offering is received. As the water ripples in concentric circles toward the outer reaches of the pool, so too this word enlarges and embraces, in love, each member of the circle.

Faith-sharing groups are usually made up of seven to ten members who gather at a prearranged time and place. One member designated as the leader calls the group to prayer and invites them to some moments of silence, during which they pray for the presence of the Holy Spirit. The leader gathers their silent prayer in an opening prayer, spontaneous or prepared.

One of the members reads a previously chosen Scripture passage on which participants have spent some time in solitary prayer. A period of silence follows each reading of the Scripture. Then the leader invites each person to share a word or phrase from the reading. Another member rereads the passage; this is followed by a time of silence.

The leader invites those members who desire to share how this passage personally affects them—whether, for example, it challenges, comforts, or inspires them.

Again the passage is read. Members are invited to offer their spontaneous prayers. Finally, the leader draws the time of faith sharing to a close with a prayer, a blessing, an Our Father, or a hymn. Before the group disbands, the passage for the following session is announced.

## 3. The Role of Imagination in Prayer

Imagination is our power of memory and recall, which makes it possible for us to enter the experience of the past and to create the future. Through images we are able to touch the center of who we are and to give life and expression to the innermost levels of our being.

The use of images is important to our development, both spiritually and psychologically. Images simultaneously reveal multiple levels of meaning and are therefore symbolic of a deeper reality. Through the structured use of active imagination, we release the hidden energy and potential to become the complete person that God has created us to be.

When active imagination is used in the context of prayer, and *with an attitude of faith*, we open ourselves to the power and mystery of God's transforming presence within us. Because Scripture is, for the most part, a collection of stories and rich in sensual imagery, the use of active imagination in praying Scripture is particularly enriching. When we rely on images as we read Scripture, we go beyond the truth of history to discover the truth of the mystery of God's creative word in our lives (12, p. 76).

## 4. Coping with Distractions

It is important not to become overly concerned or discouraged by distractions during prayer. Simply put them aside and return to your prayer material. If and when a distraction persists, it may be a call to attend prayerfully to the object of distraction. For example, it would not be surprising if an unresolved conflict continues to surface until you have dealt with it.

## Part One

# God's Love

## Week One, Day 1

# God's Encircling Presence

........................................................................

### PSALM 139:1–18

O LORD, you have searched me and known me.
You know when I sit down and when I rise up;
    you discern my thoughts from far away.
You search out my path and my lying down,
    and are acquainted with all my ways.
Even before a word is on my tongue,
    O LORD, you know it completely.
You hem me in, behind and before,
    and lay your hand upon me.
Such knowledge is too wonderful for me;
    it is so high that I cannot attain it.

Where can I go from your spirit?
    Or where can I flee from your presence?
If I ascend to heaven, you are there;
    if I make my bed in Sheol, you are there.
If I take the wings of the morning
    and settle at the farthest limits of the sea,
even there your hand shall lead me,
    and your right hand shall hold me fast.
If I say, "Surely the darkness shall cover me,
    and the light around me become night,"
even the darkness is not dark to you;

the night is as bright as the day,
    for darkness is as light to you.


For it was you who formed my inward parts;
    you knit me together in my mother's womb.
I praise you, for I am fearfully and wonderfully made.
    Wonderful are your works;
that I know very well.
    My frame was not hidden from you,
when I was being made in secret,
    intricately woven in the depths of the earth.
Your eyes beheld my unformed substance.
In your book were written
    all the days that were formed for me,
    when none of them as yet existed.
How weighty to me are your thoughts, O God!
    How vast is the sum of them!
I try to count them—they are more than the sand;
    I come to the end—I am still with you.

## Commentary

PSALM 139 CALLS US TO one of the most precious insights conceivable: the experience of ourselves as a divine "secret." Scholars are not certain of the psalmist's intent. The psalm may be a hymn of thanksgiving. It may even have been a defense; some scholars speculate that it was composed by a religious leader accused of worshipping false gods. What is obvious is that it is a consideration of God's pervasive, pursuing presence, shaped not in impersonal terms but in concrete images drawn from the life experience of the poet.

The psalmist stands before God. In the opening verses, he is aware of the penetrating gaze of God, who knows the psalmist's very heart and soul. It is the gaze of the physician, diagnostic and incisive, probing and discerning the evasive but death-dealing symptoms of disease. It is the look of the mentor who perceives the hidden potential within the student and is sensitive to the inner drive of unrealized dreams. It is the mother's contemplation of her child, the love-knowledge of a creator for that which has been formed in the embrace of love.

"O Lord, you have searched me and known me." The poet is aware of God's inescapable presence. Like the atmospheric shield that encircles our planet, God's presence is everywhere. God shows his face in the depths of despair as well as in the heights of joy. He meets us at every crossroads, even in the dark recesses of our unfaithfulness. There is no escape. So great a love demands a total response.

"Where can I flee from your presence?" The poet looks into his own heart and reverently contemplates the marvel of God's creative action, not only in the womb of his mother but also in his personal history. The hands of God have been knitting him together, leading him through the various stages of his life, and they have brought him to this moment.

# Suggested Approach to Prayer: God in My Life

## Daily Prayer Pattern (refer to pages 1–3).
I quiet myself and relax in the presence of God.
I declare my dependence on God.

## Grace

I ask for the gift of trust and confidence in God's love and for a readiness to let God teach me to pray.

## Method

I review my life and write down twelve significant events of my life from my birth until the present time.

1. ......................................................................................................

......................................................................................................

2. ......................................................................................................

......................................................................................................

3. ......................................................................................................

......................................................................................................

4. ......................................................................................................

......................................................................................................

5. ......................................................................................................

......................................................................................................

6. ......................................................................................................

......................................................................................................

7. ......................................................................................................

......................................................................................................

8. ......................................................................................................

......................................................................................................

9. ....................................................................................................

....................................................................................................

10. ....................................................................................................

....................................................................................................

11. ....................................................................................................

....................................................................................................

12. ....................................................................................................

....................................................................................................

How has God's love been present and revealed to me at each of these events?

> I focus on one event; I remember the time and imaginatively re-create and enter into the scene of the event:
>
> Where am I in the scene? What kind of day was it?
>
> What did I feel? Joy? Delight? Any other emotion?
>
> Who were the people involved?
>
> I let the feelings that I experienced then be present to me now.

I pray Psalm 139. I let the words wash over me. I open myself to receive God's love. I allow his presence to enter and to fill me.
I thank God for being present within my history.
I close my prayer with the Our Father.

## Review of Prayer

I record in my journal the event I focused on and the feelings and reflections I experienced.

# Week One, Day 2

# You Are Precious

..............................................................................................

### Isaiah 43:1–7

But now thus says the Lord,

    he who created you, O Jacob,

    he who formed you, O Israel:

Do not fear, for I have redeemed you;

    I have called you by name, you are mine.

When you pass through the waters, I will be with you;

    and through the rivers, they shall not overwhelm you;

when you walk through fire you shall not be burned,

and the flame shall not consume you.

    For I am the Lord your God,

    the Holy One of Israel, your Savior.

I give Egypt as your ransom,

    Ethiopia and Seba in exchange for you.

Because you are precious in my sight,

    and honored, and I love you,

I give people in return for you,

    nations in exchange for your life.

Do not fear, for I am with you;

    I will bring your offspring from the east,

    and from the west I will gather you;

I will say to the north, "Give them up,"
and to the south, "Do not withhold;
bring my sons from far away
and my daughters from the end of the earth—
everyone who is called by my name,
whom I created for my glory,
whom I formed and made.

## Commentary

IN THIS PASSAGE, GOD DIRECTLY addresses his people, the Israelites, through the words of Isaiah, the poet and prophet. It is helpful in reading these verses to have some sense of the historical references. God's people carry the name of their ancestor Jacob, who was given the name Israel by God (Genesis 32:23–32). The passage through the sea may be a reference to the saving event of the Exodus through the Red Sea (Exodus 14). Strongly yet tenderly, the Lord speaks to his people and reminds them of his love, not only in the formation of the nation of Israel but also as a sustaining presence throughout the perils of their history.

In the passage, God directly addresses the fear of his people. In the timelessness of God's word, we, the new Israel, are reassured in the midst of the perils of our lives and our times.

Fire and water were, to early Israel, ever-present and realistic threats. In the face of fire, there was no recourse, no help. People were at the mercy of flames as fire swept through a village, destroying every home. Never a seafaring people, the Israelites also had a deep fear of the sea's dark mysteries.

Primordially, water and fire are symbols grounded deeply in our human psyche. Paradoxically, they are representative of danger and death as well as of cleansing, new life, power, and energy. The images of fire and water engender responses not only of fear and anxiety but also of hope.

As the Old Testament word is spoken today, in our personal lives and in society, where do we experience the passage through the sea and the walk through fire?

"Do not fear, for I am with you." With unerring accuracy, this passage identifies our most vulnerable weakness: fear, fear of being unloved and unlovable. To each of us, whenever we are in the throes of that fear, the Lord says: "I have called you by name . . . you are mine . . . you are precious in my eyes . . . I love you . . . I am with you."

In the midst of their fear-filled experiences, the Israelites heard these incredibly reassuring words of God. In our own lives, we often discover that the Lord's favorite time and place to speak are during these same kinds of experiences!

# Suggested Approach to Prayer: A Love Letter from God

## Daily Prayer Pattern
I quiet myself and relax in the presence of God.
I declare my dependence on God.

## Grace
I ask for a deep experience of God's care, goodness, kindness, and faithfulness to me.

## Method: Meditation (refer to page 6)

The word of God is a word of love addressed to us during the difficulties and trials of our lives:

> I approach Isaiah 43 as God's personal love letter to me. I allow his reassuring words to enter into my heart.
>
> I let the words wash over me. I stay with those words or phrases that have particularly touched me.
>
> I talk quietly to God in my own words, thanking him for his word of love.
>
> I close my prayer with an Our Father.

## Review of Prayer

I write in my journal any feelings, experiences, or insights that have come to my awareness during this prayer period.

Week One, Day 3

# God First Loved Us

.................................................................................

## 1 John 4:7–8, 18–19

Beloved, let us love one another, because love is from God; everyone who loves is born of God and knows God. Whoever does not love does not know God, for God is love. There is no fear in love, but perfect love casts out fear; for fear has to do with punishment, and whoever fears has not reached perfection in love. We love because he first loved us.

## Commentary

GOD IS LOVE. HOW EASILY we say it; how often we hear it. How do we penetrate a phrase that is, in so many ways, a cliché? St. John reaches out to guide us toward a greater understanding of, and openness to, that love.

John tells us that the origin of all love is in God and that human love is a reflection of God's love. He assures us that God's love is a creative force, a love that has called into being all of creation—each one of us! We are invited to receive and to return love.

God's love is an effective love. It changes us—our way of seeing and our way of responding. Although we cannot see God, we can see the effect of his love in the circumstances of our lives. His love becomes visible in an awareness of his caring for us through all the people who have loved us. It becomes visible in the realization of the many times we have been spared the consequences of our sin and foolishness.

Most of all, God's love becomes visible when we feel our fears dissipating and our hearts expanding with love and concern for others. Even if our personal experiences of being loved have sometimes been disappointing, there is within the core of us, always alive, always yearning, the Spirit of love, the Spirit of God, which continues to create us and to hold us in being.

God is love; he has first loved us.

# Suggested Approach to Prayer: A Window on God

## Daily Prayer Pattern
I quiet myself and relax in the presence of God.
I declare my dependence on God.

## Grace
I ask for an experience of God's care, goodness, kindness, and faithfulness to me.

## Method
My image of God has been formed by experience. My life reflects the image I hold in my heart. The image is not fixed; it is ever growing toward fullness.

I will use the following exercise as a window on God, to see more clearly who God is for me. Use this space for feelings, insights, questions, or resolutions that emerge from your reflection on the other three areas:

| | |
|---|---|
| God—as he was presented to me, or taught to me, when I was a child | |
| God—as I would like to know him; as I would like him to be; as I would like to relate to him | |
| God—as I have come to know him through my own experience and searching | |

I close with the Our Father.

## Review of Prayer

I write in my journal about any new awareness of how God has been a sustaining presence throughout my personal journey.

## Week One, Day 4

# Love Made Visible

．．．．．．．．．．．．．．．．．．．．．．．．．．．．．．．．．．．．．．．．．．．．．．．．．．．．．．．．．．．．．．．．．．．．．．．．．．．．．．．．．．．．．．．．

### EXODUS 19:3–4

Then Moses went up to God; the LORD called to him from the mountain, saying, "Thus you shall say to the house of Jacob, and tell the Israelites: You have seen what I did to the Egyptians, and how I bore you on eagles' wings and brought you to myself."

## Commentary

AFTER THREE MONTHS IN THE desert, the Israelites came to an oasis. They pitched camp facing the mountain. From that mountain, Moses and his people received an astonishing offer: the God who led them out of slavery offered them an invitation into a relationship of freedom. He gave them the choice to love, and that choice was based on what they had experienced of his love—an unfailing faithfulness.

This faithful presence of God was experienced not only in their deliverance from the Reed Sea but also in his caring for them in the desert. The ancient symbol of the eagle is used to express to the Israelites God's presence and power; he will be with them, even carrying them on the journey.

While the description of the offer may seem legalistic and formal, what God was really offering the Israelites was a relationship of love. I will be your God, and you shall be my people (Leviticus 26:12). This love was not unlike a marriage between two people. The contract was formal and legally binding, but the commitment was one of love. In choosing to love each other, a uniquely intimate union is created—a union that will sustain and support them.

Like the Israelites, we too receive this astonishing offer. Insofar as we say yes, the promise—the covenant—is fulfilled, and we become God's own people, a priestly people, holy and consecrated.

# Suggested Approach to Prayer: An Astonishing Offer

## Daily Prayer Pattern
I quiet myself and relax in the presence of God.
I declare my dependence on God.

## Grace
I ask for the gift of experiencing God's care, goodness, kindness, and faithfulness to me.

## Method: "Your eyes saw what I did" (Joshua 24:7)
I reflect how, in my life history, I have been "carried" and sustained by the love I have received.

I recall the many ways in which this love was made visible—through the provision of my physical needs, through supportive relationships, through the enjoyment of life and a sense of purpose.

I become aware that these gifts have been a part of God's plan for me. I allow myself to experience the security and freedom of God's particular care and choice of me.

In light of this experience of all God has done for me, I imagine and record in my journal how the commitment God has offered me might appear if written. For example:

"I, God, as your creator, do hereby agree to love you unconditionally. I will manifest this love within the circumstances and reality of your life in the following ways:

I will support you by .............................................................

..........................................................................................

I will nourish you by ...........................................................

..........................................................................................

I will give you ......................................................................

..........................................................................................

I will ....................................................................................

..........................................................................................

The conditions of this commitment have been effective from the moment of my first thought of you. This offer is exempt from ever being terminated.

Signed, GOD"

I close my prayer with the Our Father.

## Week One, Day 5

# Tender, Kind, and Compassionate

········································································

### PSALM 103

Bless the LORD, O my soul,
  and all that is within me,
  bless his holy name.
Bless the LORD, O my soul,
  and do not forget all his benefits—
who forgives all your iniquity,
  who heals all your diseases,
who redeems your life from the Pit,
  who crowns you with steadfast love and mercy,
who satisfies you with good as long as you live
  so that your youth is renewed like the eagle's.

The LORD works vindication
  and justice for all who are oppressed.
He made known his ways to Moses,
  his acts to the people of Israel.
The LORD is merciful and gracious,
  slow to anger and abounding in steadfast love.
He will not always accuse,
  nor will he keep his anger forever.
He does not deal with us according to our sins,
  nor repay us according to our iniquities.

For as the heavens are high above the earth,
  so great is his steadfast love toward those who fear him;
as far as the east is from the west,
  so far he removes our transgressions from us.
As a father has compassion for his children,
  so the LORD has compassion for those who fear him.
For he knows how we were made;
  he remembers that we are dust.

As for mortals, their days are like grass;
  they flourish like a flower of the field;
for the wind passes over it, and it is gone,
  and its place knows it no more.
But the steadfast love of the LORD is from everlasting to everlasting
  on those who fear him,
  and his righteousness to children's children,
to those who keep his covenant
  and remember to do his commandments.

The LORD has established his throne in the heavens,
  and his kingdom rules over all.
Bless the LORD, O you his angels,
  you mighty ones who do his bidding,
  obedient to his spoken word.
Bless the LORD, all his hosts,
  his ministers that do his will.
Bless the LORD, all his works,
  in all places of his dominion.
Bless the LORD, O my soul.

# Commentary

THIS PSALM IS AN OLD Testament magnificat, a hymn of praise and thanksgiving. In its beauty, it is an encompassing theological statement that comes alive in the unique and profound depth of the psalmist's personal spirituality. It is liturgically expressed in song and was probably sung by an individual rather than a choir. The reference to God as king suggests that the setting was the festival of the Lord's enthronement at the beginning of the new year.

In this psalm we have one of the clearest descriptions of an individual's relationship to God. The psalmist recounts to us how he experiences God in relationship to himself, to his people Israel, and to all of creation. The psalm reveals to us a God who is near, yet transcendent, loving, and faithful. God is as near as our next breath. He is present in the healing of our brokenness, in the forgiving of our sins, and in the joy of our tender sharing with one another. Just as the molting eagle receives new feathers for flight, we too receive all that we need.

Standing among his own people, the psalmist recalls that God's love revealed the covenant offered through Moses on the mountain of Sinai. This covenant was one of everlasting mercy. The word used here is *hesed*, the Hebrew word that embraces the fullness of a love that is totally kind, tender, and compassionate. Such love is a gift, undeserved and unconditional.

The psalmist reassures us that, although we, as human creatures, are frail and live for only a brief time, the fullness of our existence is realized within the faithfulness of God's love for us. We need only surrender ourselves in trust.

Finally, the psalmist tells us that God embraces not only all of humanity but also all of creation. He is Lord of heaven and earth. May he be Lord of each human heart.

# Suggested Approach to Prayer: The Energy of Love

## Daily Prayer Pattern

I quiet myself and relax in the presence of God.

I declare my dependence on God.

## Grace

I ask for the grace to experience God's care, goodness, kindness, and faithfulness to me.

## Method: Meditation

I read the psalm slowly, several times. As I read, I breathe in the tender, kind, and understanding love of God. I imagine the strength of this love flowing through me. Just as my arteries deliver the sustenance of life to every cell and synapse of my body, God's sustaining love permeates my entire being.

I allow myself to experience the energizing refreshment that this love brings.

I close with the Our Father.

## Review of Prayer

I write in my journal any feelings, experiences, or insights that have come to my awareness during this prayer period.

# Week One, Day 6

# Repetition

## Suggested Approach to Prayer

### Daily Prayer Pattern

I quiet myself and relax in the presence of God.
I declare my dependence on God.

### Grace

I ask for the grace to experience God's care, goodness, kindness, and faithfulness to me.

### Method

It will be particularly helpful to read "Repetition" on pages 7 and 8.

In preparation I review my prayer by reading my journal of the past week. I select for my repetition the period of prayer in which I was deeply moved by joy, gratitude, or awe. I proceed in the manner I did originally, focusing on the scene, word, or feeling that was significant.

### Review of Prayer

I write in my journal any feelings, experiences, or insights that have come to my awareness during this prayer period.

# Part Two

## God's Goodness

# Week Two, Day 1
# With Cords of Kindness

## HOSEA 11:1–9

When Israel was a child, I loved him,
  and out of Egypt I called my son.
The more I called them,
  the more they went from me;
they kept sacrificing to the Baals,
  and offering incense to idols.

Yet it was I who taught Ephraim to walk,
  I took them up in my arms;
  but they did not know that I healed them.
I led them with cords of human kindness,
  with bands of love.
I was to them like those
  who lift infants to their cheeks.
  I bent down to them and fed them.

They shall return to the land of Egypt,
  and Assyria shall be their king,
  because they have refused to return to me.
The sword rages in their cities,
  it consumes their oracle-priests,
  and devours because of their schemes.

My people are bent on turning away from me.
>> To the Most High they call,
>> but he does not raise them up at all.

How can I give you up, Ephraim?
>> How can I hand you over, O Israel?
How can I make you like Admah?
>> How can I treat you like Zeboiim?
My heart recoils within me;
>> my compassion grows warm and tender.
I will not execute my fierce anger;
>> I will not again destroy Ephraim;
for I am God and no mortal,
>> the Holy One in your midst,
>> and I will not come in wrath.

## Commentary

ONE OF THE TENDER IMAGES of this passage is "bands of love": in the context of a nomadic existence in which many dangers existed both inside and outside the camp, parents might use a harness and leash to attach a toddler to the family tent. This would keep the child from wandering off or getting too close to the open fire pit. It was truly "a cord of kindness." One can imagine a parent also using that leash to draw the child in for frequent hugs and care.

All parents know how difficult and painful it is to discipline their children with "tough love." Our God experiences pain, even agony, in allowing his wayward people to experience the harsh reality that is the consequence of their unfaithfulness.

Hosea gives us a glimpse into the heart of God as he reveals the Lord's persistent effort in establishing a love relationship with Israel. Throughout the passage, we witness the parentlike concern on the part of God and the constant resistance on the part of Israel.

In the words of Hosea, we see how tenderly God nurtured Israel, taught him to walk, guided him, held him to his cheek. Yet the more God called, the farther away Israel moved, seeking security through political alliances with Egypt and Assyria that could be found only in God.

God's patience is exhausted, and his anger erupts! He says in effect: "Have your own way. Go to Egypt. Accept the consequences!" Parents can identify with and understand God's angry response. They can relate to God's poignant sense of loss and fear for his people as they catapult toward disaster.

"How can I hand you over? . . . My heart recoils within me; my compassion grows warm and tender."

God's mercy prevails. Even in Israel's deepest rejection of God, and though he deserves his harshest punishment, he does not cease to love Israel. This is a love surpassing our human understanding, a love that encompasses both judgment and hope.

Such is God's love. We feel it not only in the sweetness of consolation but also in the darkness of discipline. That darkness is, as the poet Francis Thompson says, "the shadow of his hand outstretched caressingly" (30, p. 60).

# Suggested Approach to Prayer: Loved and Forgiven

## Daily Prayer Pattern

I quiet myself and relax in the presence of God.

I declare my dependence on God.

## Grace

I ask for the grace to realize that I am totally accepted, to sense the unconditional love of the Father, and the presence of God as a gift and not a threat.

## Method: Contemplation (refer to pages 4 and 5)

I recall a time when I experienced being forgiven—of being loved even when I was most resistant. In my imagination, I place myself in that situation. I gently recall it in detail. I allow myself to experience the feelings that accompanied being accepted and forgiven.

In remembering, how am I aware of God's love expressed within the human situation?

I close my prayer with an Our Father.

## Review of Prayer

I write in my journal any feelings, experiences, or insights that have come to my awareness during this prayer period.

## Week Two, Day 2

# From Fear to Confidence

............................................................................................

### LUKE 12:4–7

I tell you, my friends, do not fear those who kill the body, and after that can do nothing more. But I will warn you whom to fear: fear him who, after he has killed, has authority to cast into hell. Yes, I tell you, fear him! Are not five sparrows sold for two pennies? Yet not one of them is forgotten in God's sight. But even the hairs of your head are all counted. Do not be afraid; you are of more value than many sparrows.

## Commentary

"DO NOT BE AFRAID." THE frequency of those words in Scripture indicates the great need we all have of being reassured that God loves us and cares for us.

It has been said that fear is the devil's greatest tool. In the preceding verses, Jesus has instructed his disciples about the evil of hypocrisy. Hypocrites are those who present themselves dishonestly. They need constantly to justify themselves and live up to a reputation. The root of hypocrisy is fear—fear of what others will say or think. It is basically a fear of being unlovable, and therefore a fear of being rejected.

Jesus tells his disciples not to fear because there is a limit to the power others have over them. Even if our hypocrisy were to buy some measure of security with others, the price of denying our true selves would eventually plunge us into the hell of our own emptiness. God would be absent, and that is hell.

What we need to fear, then, is only the absence of God in our lives. To the one who has this kind of fear, Jesus says, "You are unconditionally accepted."

These words from Jesus call us to make the leap from fear to confidence. It is a confidence that places our lives in the hands of a love so great that not even a sparrow, or the least anxiety, or the shortest moment, or one blade of grass, or a single hair on our head, is insignificant.

# Suggested Approach to Prayer: A Letter of Encouragement

## Daily Prayer Pattern

I quiet myself and relax in the presence of God.
I declare my dependence on God.

## Grace

I ask for the grace to realize that I am totally accepted by God, to sense the unconditional love and presence of God as a gift and not a threat.

## Method: Meditation

I receive and prayerfully read this passage as if it were a letter from Jesus addressed personally to me.

In response to these reassuring words of Christ, I allow all my anxieties to be dissipated, and I open myself to be filled with confidence. I imagine the evil spirit of fear giving way to God's spirit of courage.

I close my prayer with the Our Father.

## Review of Prayer

I write in my journal any feelings, experiences, or insights that have come to my awareness during this prayer period.

## Week Two, Day 3

# Held in Remembrance

....................................................................................

### ISAIAH 49:14–16

But Zion said, "The LORD has forsaken me,
 my Lord has forgotten me."
Can a woman forget her nursing child,
 or show no compassion for the child of her womb?
Even these may forget,
 yet I will not forget you.
See, I have inscribed you on the palms of my hands;
 your walls are continually before me.

## Commentary

THIS IS ONE OF THE most touching expressions of God's love. It affirms the unbroken union of Yahweh and his people. Upon entering a relationship, our greatest fear is that the one who loves us will forget us. To be forgotten is to be abandoned, to be lost. It really is not true that it is better to have loved and lost than never to have loved at all. There is nothing more painful than to lose love.

We are assured of God's everlasting faithfulness in the beautiful imagery of the love of a mother for her child. When her child is grown, a mother remembers. She remembers the first word, the first step. In remembering, she continues to give life. Even if a mother in her human weakness would fail to remember, God will not forget.

The words of this passage were addressed to the Israelite people at a time of political upheaval and amid the uncertainties of exile. They were announced as part of the promise of God's continual faithfulness. Israel needed to be comforted by these words of Isaiah.

The message of this passage knows no age. God will never abandon us, his precious children. There will never be any circumstance or sin that will nullify this love. God's creative and nurturing love of us continues. *I have inscribed you on the palms of my hands.* We are secure in God's remembering us.

# Suggested Approach to Prayer: A Child Is Born

## Daily Prayer Pattern

I quiet myself and relax in the presence of God.
I declare my dependence on God.

## Grace

I ask for the gift of experiencing the total acceptance of God, who loves me unconditionally; I beg for a deeper longing for God.

## Method: Contemplation

I imagine myself as a mother or father.

In my imagination, I move through the waiting period of the pregnancy, my child's birth, and the early years of his or her childhood. I begin with the moment when I first learn of the pregnancy: the excitement and anticipation, the birth, the first time I hold my son or daughter, the first step, the first word.

In memory and imagination, I am aware of my maternal or paternal feelings—the excitement, joy, and tenderness.

I reread the passage. I listen to God speak to me as his child.

I close my prayer with the Our Father.

## Review of Prayer

I write in my journal any feelings, experiences, or insights that have come to my awareness during this prayer period.

## Week Two, Day 4
# God's Kindness Forever

.......................................................................

### PSALM 136: LITANY OF THANKSGIVING

O give thanks to the LORD, for he is good,
    for his steadfast love endures forever.
O give thanks to the God of gods,
    for his steadfast love endures forever.
O give thanks to the Lord of lords,
    for his steadfast love endures forever;

who alone does great wonders,
    for his steadfast love endures forever;
who by understanding made the heavens,
    for his steadfast love endures forever;
who spread out the earth on the waters,
    for his steadfast love endures forever;
who made the great lights,
    for his steadfast love endures forever;
the sun to rule over the day,
    for his steadfast love endures forever;
the moon and stars to rule over the night,
    for his steadfast love endures forever;

who struck Egypt through their firstborn,
    for his steadfast love endures forever;

and brought Israel out from among them,

    for his steadfast love endures forever;

with a strong hand and an outstretched arm,

    for his steadfast love endures forever;

who divided the Red Sea in two,

    for his steadfast love endures forever;

and made Israel pass through the midst of it,

    for his steadfast love endures forever;

but overthrew Pharaoh and his army in the Red Sea,

    for his steadfast love endures forever;

who led his people through the wilderness,

    for his steadfast love endures forever;

who struck down great kings,

    for his steadfast love endures forever;

and killed famous kings,

    for his steadfast love endures forever;

Sihon, king of the Amorites,

    for his steadfast love endures forever;

and Og, king of Bashan,

    for his steadfast love endures forever;

and gave their land as a heritage,

    for his steadfast love endures forever;

a heritage to his servant Israel,

    for his steadfast love endures forever.


It is he who remembered us in our low estate,

    for his steadfast love endures forever;

and rescued us from our foes,

    for his steadfast love endures forever;

who gives food to all flesh,
  for his steadfast love endures forever.

O give thanks to the God of heaven,
  for his steadfast love endures forever.

## Commentary

THE PEOPLE ARE KNEELING, THEIR foreheads touching the ground, listening to the choir praise, in song, the wonders and goodness of God. Over and over they raise their heads to chant the response, for God's steadfast love endures forever.

The Israelites have come from their fields and villages to praise their God, to give expression to the deepest impulse in the human heart. It is the celebration of the new year, or perhaps the opening day of the Festival of Tabernacles. The place is the inner court of the temple of Jerusalem. It is a time of great celebration and heightened awareness; the temple is filled with the glory of God. This image, as described in 2 Chronicles 7, helps us grasp the profound significance of this psalm.

Liturgical in origin, this psalm is constructed as an antiphon to provide for congregational participation. The leader recites a sequence of phrases to which the congregation responds. It is, interestingly, the one psalm of the psalter that is purely liturgical throughout.

The psalmist guides the worshippers through a recollection of God's presence and action within their communal history. God's presence is celebrated in the memory of creation, the Exodus, the people's entrance into the Promised Land, the repeated deliverances of the people, and in God's continual provision for them.

The power of this psalm is that it clearly brings to consciousness the realization that every circumstance and life event is grounded in God's mercy. Only the Hebrew word *hesed* holds the tender expansiveness and loving-kindness that is God's love. Like a heartbeat, the repetitive phrase knits together, with God's love, the fragments of life and, in doing so, inspires wholeness and joy.

# Suggested Approach to Prayer: His Steadfast Love

## Daily Prayer Pattern

I quiet myself and relax in the presence of God.
I declare my dependence on God.

## Grace

I ask for the gift of experiencing deeply God's unconditional love as a presence that is never a threat and is always supportive.

## Method: Prayer Word (refer to page 6)

There are occasions when we repeat over and over a word, a name, or a phrase. In grief over the loss of a loved one, we may find ourselves repeating the name of that person, or in love we may simply repeat words of love.

I quiet myself in soul and spirit. I rest in the rhythm of God's love and my thankfulness. I repeat at comfortable intervals the words, "Your steadfast love endures forever."

I close my prayer with the Our Father.

## Review of Prayer

I write in my journal any feelings, experiences, or insights that have come to my awareness during this prayer period.

# Week Two, Day 5

# Ordained to Glory

.....................................................................................................

## PSALM 8

O LORD, our Sovereign,
how majestic is your name in all the earth!

You have set your glory above the heavens.
Out of the mouths of babes and infants
you have founded a bulwark because of your foes,
to silence the enemy and the avenger.

When I look at your heavens, the work of your fingers,
the moon and the stars that you have established;
what are human beings that you are mindful of them,
mortals that you care for them?

Yet you have made them a little lower than God,
and crowned them with glory and honor.
You have given them dominion over the works of
your hands;
you have put all things under their feet,
all sheep and oxen,
and also the beasts of the field,
the birds of the air, and the fish of the sea,
whatever passes along the paths of the seas.

O LORD, our Sovereign,

    how majestic is your name in all the earth!

# Commentary

IN JAMES MICHENER'S NOVEL *SPACE*, we share in the fascination of the young man John as he gazes into the night sky, totally captivated by the complexity, vastness, and interrelatedness of the stellar display. The novel not only portrays the beauty of space but also thrusts us forward into the promise and power it holds. The narrative revolves around the human quest for ultimate identity and meaning.

Who among us has not contemplated the night sky and been moved by its splendor? Who among us has not been humbled in the presence of such magnitude? Three thousand years ago, the psalmist expressed this same sense of awe and wonder.

If the Hebrew people discovered the presence of God in their history, they discovered his glory in nature. They had a unique capacity for feeling, and in this psalm they expressed their awesome appreciation for nature and its creator. In the attempt to express this revelation of God, the poet feels he is reduced to childish prattle. Yet, convinced that God frequently uses the lowly for his purposes, the poet lets go of his self-conscious hesitation and sings God's praise.

The God who spun stars into space has shaped with infinite care his human creatures. As insignificant as we might experience ourselves to be, we are in reality the creation with whom God most profoundly shares himself. He has given us the power to know and to love. This inestimable gift offers to each man and woman the extraordinary vocation to bring all creation into God's service.

The word of God launches us through prayer to a dependence on God that is the path to holiness.

# Suggested Approach to Prayer: The Splendor of the Night Sky

## Daily Prayer Pattern
I quiet myself and relax in the presence of God.
I declare my dependence on God.

## Grace
I ask for the grace of a sense of awe before and dependence on the love of God, who is so great, yet attends to me.

## Method: Meditation
For this prayer I treat myself to the luxury of an hour's contemplation of the stars. If this is not possible, in my imagination, I visualize and enjoy the splendor of a night sky. I allow myself to join in the psalmist's praise of God as he experiences himself as both loved and dependent on his creator.

I close my prayer with the Our Father.

## Review of Prayer
I write in my journal any feelings, experiences, or insights that have come to my awareness during this prayer period.

## Week Two, Day 6

# Repetition

......................................................................................................

## Suggested Approach to Prayer

### Daily Prayer Pattern

I quiet myself and relax in the presence of God.
I declare my dependence on God.

### Grace

I ask for the grace of a sense of awe and dependence before the love of God, who is so great, yet attends to me.

### Method: Repetition

In preparation, I review my prayer by reading my journal of the past week. I select for my repetition the period of prayer in which I was deeply moved by joy, gratitude, or awe. I proceed in the manner I did originally, focusing on the scene, word, or feeling that was most significant.

### Review of Prayer

I write in my journal any feelings, experiences, or insights that have come to my awareness during this prayer period.

## Part Three

God's Creation

## Week Three, Day 1

# On Being Resilient Clay

........................................................................................

### JEREMIAH 18:1–6

The word that came to Jeremiah from the LORD: "Come, go down to the potter's house, and there I will let you hear my words." So I went down to the potter's house, and there he was working at his wheel. The vessel he was making of clay was spoiled in the potter's hand, and he reworked it into another vessel, as seemed good to him.

Then the word of the LORD came to me: Can I not do with you, O house of Israel, just as this potter has done? says the LORD. Just like the clay in the potter's hand, so are you in my hand, O house of Israel.

## Commentary

PEOPLE HAVE BEEN MAKING POTTERY for thousands of years. This ancient craft sometimes provides the only evidence we have of a people's existence. As well as being used for practical purposes, such as food preparation and storage, pottery decoratively expresses the story of the people—of their daily life, celebrations, struggles, and beliefs.

Jeremiah frequently draws on everyday experience to illustrate to his people God's presence and action in their lives. In this passage he recalls a visit to the potter's house and tells us of the potter at work, shaping and reshaping the clay. He likens God to the potter and Israel (us) to the clay.

The quality of the clay determines the beauty of the finished vessel. If the clay is impure, it will resist the intention of the artist. The prophet suggests that this is the case with Israel. Only as the clay becomes resilient in the hands of the potter does it reach its full potential.

So it is with each of us. Only in our cooperative surrender does God have the freedom to mold us in his likeness. We do not stand outside of our being created; there is a decision, a will, a choice to be made. We are partners with God in the continual process of our development. Just as the artist and the clay have entered into a creative dynamism, God and his people have joined in the joyful experience of giving human expression and appearance to the goodness of God.

... for Christ plays in ten thousand places,
Lovely in limbs, and lovely in eyes not his
To the Father through the features of men's faces.
—Gerard Manley Hopkins (4, p. 95)

# Suggested Approach to Prayer: In the Potter's Hands

## Daily Prayer Pattern
I quiet myself and relax in the presence of God.
I declare my dependence on God.

## Grace
I ask for the gift of wonder and for a sense of my own fragility and dependence on God's love.

## Method: Contemplation

I imagine myself as clay. What color clay am I? Reddish? Gray? Yellow? What is my consistency? Dry? Malleable? Moist?

I see the hands of God, the Potter. I recall how God chose me and how he has prepared me and cleansed me of my impurities and air bubbles. I am very attentive to the Potter. Into what kind of vessel is he shaping me? As my life takes shape, I experience the dynamic tension between God's intention and my desire and responsiveness.

How does my "vessel" reflect the face, the love, the creativity, of God?

I close my prayer with the Our Father.

## Review of Prayer

I write in my journal any feelings, experiences, or insights that have come to my awareness during this prayer period.

# Week Three, Day 2

# Naked before God

·················································································································

## Job 1:20–21

Then Job arose, tore his robe, shaved his head, and fell on the ground and worshiped. He said, "Naked I came from my mother's womb, and naked shall I return there; the LORD gave, and the LORD has taken away; blessed be the name of the LORD."

## Commentary

THIS IS THE MOMENT OF Job's surrender. After having been stripped of the comfort and joy of his family and friendships and wrenched from his wealth and prestige, Job stands alone in the realization of his total dependence on God.

Job sheds his clothes and shaves his head as external expressions of his inner experience of nakedness and dependence. Job acknowledges that he came naked from his mother's womb. He knows that it is Mother Earth who will embrace him in death, even as she embraces all the rest of creation.

Bewildered, Job in his suffering and despair continues to cling to the conviction that God is as present in the taking away as he is in the giving. It is in the midst of the glaring riddle of his life that Job abandons himself in dependence and praise, declaring that God gives and God has taken back. Blessed be his name.

Traditionally, and in many cultures, these words mark the strength and courage of those who know the hands in which they ultimately rest. In our own confused and threatened world, can we be the voice of Job?

# Suggested Approach to Prayer: Prayer of Surrender

## Daily Prayer Pattern

I quiet myself and relax in the presence of God.
I declare my dependence on God.

## Grace

I ask for the grace of wonder and a sense of my own fragility and dependence on God's love.

## Method: Prayer Word

I remember a time when I, like Job, felt stripped and emptied. I recall those times when I experienced a loss, such as the death of a loved one, unemployment, a ruptured relationship, or a loss of reputation.

Retrospectively, I ponder how God was present in this painful experience of loss. I bring to my awareness the areas in which I now experience the lack or loss of something meaningful.

Holding the experience in my heart, I pray using a repetitive prayer word, taken from either of Job's prayers.

Naked I came from my mother's womb, and
naked shall I return there.
The LORD gave, and the LORD has taken away;
blessed be the name of the LORD.

I say the first part of the prayer while inhaling, and the second phrase while exhaling. I let the spirit of the words fill my emptiness.

I close my prayer with the Our Father.

## Review of Prayer

I write in my journal any feelings, experiences, or insights that have come to my awareness during this prayer period.

Week Three, Day 3

# The Splendor of God

........................................................................

## PSALM 104

Bless the LORD, O my soul.
    O LORD my God, you are very great.
You are clothed with honor and majesty,
    wrapped in light as with a garment.
You stretch out the heavens like a tent,
    you set the beams of your chambers on the waters,
you make the clouds your chariot,
    you ride on the wings of the wind,
you make the winds your messengers,
    fire and flame your ministers.

You set the earth on its foundations,
    so that it shall never be shaken.
You cover it with the deep as with a garment;
    the waters stood above the mountains.
At your rebuke they flee;
    at the sound of your thunder they take to flight.
They rose up to the mountains, ran down to the valleys
    to the place that you appointed for them.
You set a boundary that they may not pass,
    so that they might not again cover the earth.

You make springs gush forth in the valleys;
  they flow between the hills,
giving drink to every wild animal;
  the wild asses quench their thirst.
By the streams the birds of the air have their habitation;
  they sing among the branches.
From your lofty abode you water the mountains;
  the earth is satisfied with the fruit of your work.


You cause the grass to grow for the cattle,
  and plants for people to use,
to bring forth food from the earth,
  and wine to gladden the human heart,
oil to make the face shine,
  and bread to strengthen the human heart.
The trees of the LORD are watered abundantly,
  the cedars of Lebanon that he planted.
In them the birds build their nests;
  the stork has its home in the fir trees.
The high mountains are for the wild goats;
  the rocks are a refuge for the coneys.
You have made the moon to mark the seasons;
  the sun knows its time for setting.
You make darkness, and it is night,
  when all the animals of the forest come creeping out.
The young lions roar for their prey,
  seeking their food from God.
When the sun rises, they withdraw
  and lie down in their dens.

People go out to their work
    and to their labor until the evening.

O Lord, how manifold are your works!
    In wisdom you have made them all;
    the earth is full of your creatures.
Yonder is the sea, great and wide,
    creeping things innumerable are there,
    living things both small and great.
There go the ships,
    and Leviathan that you formed to sport in it.

These all look to you
    to give them their food in due season;
when you give to them, they gather it up;
    when you open your hand, they are filled with good things.
When you hide your face, they are dismayed;
    when you take away their breath, they die
    and return to their dust.
When you send forth your spirit, they are created;
    and you renew the face of the ground.

May the glory of the Lord endure forever;
    may the Lord rejoice in his works—
who looks on the earth and it trembles,
    who touches the mountains and they smoke.
I will sing to the Lord as long as I live;
    I will sing praise to my God while I have being.

May my meditation be pleasing to him,
> for I rejoice in the LORD.

Let sinners be consumed from the earth,
> and let the wicked be no more.

Bless the LORD, O my soul.

Praise the LORD!

# Commentary

AS YOU ARE READING THIS, the very breath you are inhaling is directly dependent on God's goodness and love for you. This total dependence—our dependence, the dependence of all creation—is the essence and heart of this psalm.

With beautiful words the poet weaves a picture of all creation. The tapestry of images carries us on a journey from the primeval waters with mythical sea dragons into the present age of our planet. God's sustaining love and power continue to create and maintain all creatures in an interdependent, interconnected system.

As with many of the psalms, this psalm has its literary roots in the mythology of the ancient world. The poet was familiar with the Babylonian creation myth: the destruction of the dragon of disorder so that an orderly world could emerge.

Scholars also point out that this psalm carries an Egyptian influence. It appears to reflect something of the hymn to the Egyptian sun god, Aton. For the Egyptians, the sun was a symbol for God. The psalmist, however, true to his Hebraic tradition, describes the sun being taught by God.

Throughout the psalm, dependence on God is emphasized, and in the last verses, this dependence is expressed in the poet's personal reflections. Life and death are intimately contingent on God's faithful presence and care.

When you hide your face, they are dismayed;
> when you take away their breath, they die and return to their
> > dust.
When you send forth your spirit, they are created.

# Suggested Approach to Prayer: God's Creative Power

## Daily Prayer Pattern
I quiet myself and relax in the presence of God.
I declare my dependence on God.

## Grace
I ask for the gift of wonder and a sense of my own fragility and dependence on God's love.

## Method: Meditation
I read Psalm 104 slowly. When one particular image attracts me, I ponder it. I let it become distinct, and I see it in detail. I use all my senses to bring it to life.

Then I imagine that I am the wind, the spring, the trees, one of the animals, or whatever image first attracted me in the psalm. I see the rest of creation from within the perspective of this image.

I rest within the creative energy of God who brought it forth, just as he has created me. I allow it to fill me with God's power.

I close with the prayer: "Glory be to the Father, and to the Son, and to the Holy Spirit; as it was in the beginning, is now, and ever shall be, world without end. Amen."

## Review of Prayer

I write in my journal any feelings, experiences, or insights that have come to my awareness during this prayer period.

# Week Three, Day 4
# The Language of Love

····················································································

## Psalm 19

The heavens are telling the glory of God;
    and the firmament proclaims his handiwork.
Day to day pours forth speech,
    and night to night declares knowledge.
There is no speech, nor are there words;
    their voice is not heard;
yet their voice goes out through all the earth,
    and their words to the end of the world.

In the heavens he has set a tent for the sun,
    which comes out like a bridegroom from his wedding canopy,
    and like a strong man runs its course with joy.
Its rising is from the end of the heavens,
    and its circuit to the end of them;
    and nothing is hid from its heat.

The law of the LORD is perfect,
    reviving the soul;
the decrees of the LORD are sure,
    making wise the simple;
the precepts of the LORD are right,
    rejoicing the heart;

the commandment of the LORD is clear,
    enlightening the eyes;
the fear of the LORD is pure,
    enduring forever;
the ordinances of the LORD are true
    and righteous altogether.
More to be desired are they than gold,
    even much fine gold;
sweeter also than honey,
    and drippings of the honeycomb.

Moreover by them is your servant warned;
    in keeping them there is great reward.
But who can detect their errors?
    Clear me from hidden faults.
Keep back your servant also from the insolent;
    do not let them have dominion over me.
Then I shall be blameless,
    and innocent of great transgression.

Let the words of my mouth and the meditation of my heart
    be acceptable to you,
    O LORD, my rock and my redeemer.

# Commentary

IMAGINE YOURSELF AS JUST HAVING arrived in a strange country. You don't know the language so you can't ask for directions or read the signs, and you don't understand the words of people who are trying to talk with you. You feel frustrated and lost.

Through persistence, you eventually arrive at your hotel room. Upon reflection, you realize that communication occurred that was not dependent on the spoken word. Communication took place through a jumble of expressions: smiles, shrugs, pointing, frowns. Although it was frustrating, through it all you also felt somehow welcomed, directed, and understood. You even felt a small measure of security!

This example demonstrates that language is not limited to the spoken or written word. In Psalm 19, the poet shows us that the revelation of God is not limited to the spoken word.

Creation is an expression of God's love for us. Nature is God's "word" to us, and it is a word we can all understand. This word of love is available to all regardless of nationality, education, position, or status.

Nature is a universal language. Nature is a tangible reality of God's love. It speaks to us. In listening to nature, we discover a welcoming of our deepest self, a sense of direction, a release from self-preoccupation, and a growing awareness that we have a significant contribution to make to God's plan of love.

With verse 7, the psalm addresses the law of God. For the Hebrews, *law* or *Torah* refers not to isolated rules or prescriptions but to the invitation of God to his people as revealed in the stories of the first five books of the Old Testament. The stories are about creation, sin, healing, and God's special choice of the Hebrew people. The stories reveal God's law as a declaration of his love.

In our own stories—our creation, our sin, our healing, and God's special choice of us—God continues to speak his word and law of love. When we embrace our strengths and our weaknesses, our light and our darkness, we embrace the reality of our total selves and become whole. When we are united with ourselves, we are united with our Creator and with all things created. Only in such surrender do we realize true joy and give glory to God.

# Suggested Approach to Prayer: A Rose

## Daily Prayer Pattern

I quiet myself and relax in the presence of God.

I declare my dependence on God.

## Grace

I ask for the gift of wonder and awe, and a sense of my own fragility and dependence on God's love.

## Method: Contemplation

Imagine a rosebush: roots, stem, leaves, and on top, a rosebud. The rosebud is closed and enveloped by its green sepals. Take time to visualize all the details clearly.

Now imagine that the sepals start to open, turn back, and reveal the petals inside—tender, delicate, still closed.

Now the petals themselves slowly begin to open. As they do so, you become aware of a blossoming also occurring in the depths of your being. You feel that something in you is opening and coming to light.

As you keep visualizing the rose, you feel that its rhythm is your rhythm, its opening is your opening. You keep watching the rose as it opens up to the light and the air, as it reveals itself in all its beauty.

You smell its perfume and absorb it into yourself.

Now gaze into the very center of the rose, where its life is most intense. Let an image emerge from there. This image represents what is most beautiful, most meaningful, and most creative that wants to come to light in your life right now. It can be an image of absolutely anything. Just let it emerge spontaneously, without forcing or thinking.

Now stay with this image for some time and absorb its quality.

The image may have a message for you—a verbal or a nonverbal message. Be receptive to it.

(REPRINTED FROM *WHAT WE MAY BE*,

BY PIERO FERRUCCI; 14, PP. 132–33.)

If "the heavens are telling the glory of God," so too does each fragment of creation—so does a rose. At the end of the prayer period, pray the psalm, keeping the image of the rose before you.

I close my prayer with the Our Father.

## Review of Prayer

I write in my journal any feelings, experiences, or insights that have come to my awareness during this prayer period.

# Week Three, Day 5

# Why Me?

On the evening before, prepare for prayer by reading the commentary.

## Commentary

"WHO IS THIS WITH HIS empty-headed words?" This is God's sarcastic greeting to Job in chapters 38 and 39.

Imagine Job. He has lost everything: his health, his family, and his security. His friends' attempt to help him has resulted in greater confusion.

Job is a devout man, yet he is tormented by his anger and rage. He realizes that not only his life but also the lives of those he knows and loves are broken and sometimes filled with despair. He demands that God explain and justify the human situation of suffering and limitation that he has experienced. Job asks: "Why me? What kind of God are you?"

We can identify with the anguish of Job. Do we not cry out with the same question at times? Even if we have not lost everything, there are times when something very central to our lives collapses. It may be a personal disillusionment or the death of someone we love.

"Why me? What kind of God are you to let this happen?" And God says to us: "Who is this with his empty-headed words?" It is God's turn to ask the questions. He tells Job to "brace" himself. God does not spare Job. He puts to Job a series of questions about nature and who controls the world. The questions are utterly unanswerable, taunting, sharp, and ironic. The questions put Job's dilemma into perspective. In effect, God says to Job: "Who are you to question me or my ways?"

Who is the creator here, and who is the creature? Isn't this the question we hear addressed to us?

# Suggested Approach to Prayer: The Heart and Mind of Job

## Daily Prayer Pattern
I quiet myself and relax in the presence of God.
I declare my dependence on God.

## Grace
I ask for the grace of wonder and awe, and a sense of my fragility and dependence on God's love.

## Method: Meditative Reading (refer to page 6)
I enter into the mind and heart of Job and allow myself to sense his confusion. I slowly read chapters 38 and 39 of the book of Job. I pause periodically to allow the words and phrases to resonate within the realm of my own experience. I respond to God from the depths of my own search and longing.

I close with the Our Father.

## Review of Prayer
I write in my journal any feelings, experiences, or insights that have come to my awareness during this prayer period.

# Week Three, Day 6

# Repetition

........................................................................................................

## Suggested Approach to Prayer

### Daily Prayer Pattern

I quiet myself and relax in the presence of God.

I declare my dependence on God.

### Grace

I ask for the grace of wonder and awe before the mystery of God's creative love and my dependence on God.

### Method: Repetition

In preparation, I review my prayer by reading my journal of the past week. I select for my repetition the period of prayer in which I was most deeply moved by joy, gratitude, or awe, or perhaps a passage that did not seem to touch me at all. I proceed in the manner I did originally, opening my heart to this word of God.

### Review of Prayer

I write in my journal any feelings, experiences, or insights that have come to my awareness during this prayer period. I am particularly aware of how God may be giving me the grace I have been requesting.

## Part Four

# Spiritual Freedom

# Week Four, Day 1

# The Potter's Choice

ROMANS 9:20–21

But who indeed are you, a human being, to argue with God?
Will what is molded say to the one who molds it, "Why have
you made me like this?" Has the potter no right over the clay,
to make out of the same lump one object for special use and
another for ordinary use?

## Commentary

IMAGINE YOURSELF AS A POT sitting on a shelf in a potter's stu-
dio. You have been on this shelf for a long time, but you never
really looked at the other pottery. This morning you find yourself looking at the others in a new way, as if for the first time.

You immediately become aware of an exquisite pot on the
second shelf. It is perfectly proportioned and has been shaped of
the finest white clay. It appears flawless. In the corner you spot
a small misshapen pot and wonder why the potter hasn't dis-
carded it. It does not seem to have any redeeming qualities.

You look at both and wonder at the striking contrast between
them. Then you look at yourself and discover suddenly that you
are somewhat broken. You hadn't noticed it before, but now, as
you look closely, you see a hairline crack that extends the entire
length of yourself.

You experience panic. You question your inherent value and usefulness. Will you be able to hold anything? You feel jealous of the perfect pot. Why did the potter fail you? Was he sick the day he created you? Didn't he care?

You remember the potter. You see again his gentle face, his loving eyes, his slender, deft fingers as he selects, kneads, and shapes each lump of clay. From your position on the shelf, you have watched him for years. You know in your heart that he has never created unlovingly. Always he has "in-formed" the clay with his very own spirit. No less love has been present for the misshapen creations than for the flawless ones.

You know that at this moment you don't understand why one is perfect and another is not. What purpose do the differences serve? Perhaps you will discover your service as a broken pot. You know somehow that your value does not rest in your own degree of perfection. For now it is enough to know that you have been created—in love, of love, for love.

# Suggested Approach to Prayer: Letting Go

## Daily Prayer Pattern
I quiet myself and relax in the presence of God.
I declare my dependence on God.

## Grace
I ask for the grace of freedom, for a readiness to respond with a clear yes to whatever I am called to by God.

## Method: Contemplation

I read the commentary slowly. I imagine myself as the pot just discovering its brokenness. I ask myself the same questions the pot asked itself.

I conclude my prayer with an expression of my desire to freely submit myself to God's ongoing creation—and his purpose—for me.

Out of this stance of surrender, I pray the Our Father.

## Review of Prayer

I write in my journal any feelings, experiences, or insights that have come to my awareness during this prayer period.

# Week Four, Day 2

# Within the Fire

## Exodus 3:1–6

Moses was keeping the flock of his father-in-law Jethro, the priest of Midian; he led his flock beyond the wilderness, and came to Horeb, the mountain of God. There the angel of the LORD appeared to him in a flame of fire out of a bush; he looked, and the bush was blazing, yet it was not consumed. Then Moses said, "I must turn aside and look at this great sight, and see why the bush is not burned up." When the LORD saw that he had turned aside to see, God called to him out of the bush, "Moses, Moses!" And he said, "Here I am." Then he said, "Come no closer! Remove the sandals from your feet, for the place on which you are standing is holy ground." He said further, "I am the God of your father, the God of Abraham, the God of Isaac, and the God of Jacob." And Moses hid his face, for he was afraid to look at God.

## Commentary

MOSES IS IN THE WILDERNESS. His history, like his heart, is full of conflict. He is well established in Midian but does not feel at home there. His feelings of alienation are reflected in the name he has given his newborn son, Gershom, which means, "I am a stranger in a foreign land."

Moses's experience of alienation is one with which many of us can identify. His conflict is between who he is and who he seems to be. He finds himself in a land totally unlike Egypt, the land of his birth, from which he had to escape. He is separated not only from the Egyptian court in which he grew to manhood but also from his Hebrew roots. He was rescued as a Hebrew baby from the water by an Egyptian woman, who raised him as her son. Who is he? Where is his home?

His enforced solitude as a shepherd does not allow Moses to escape the issue. His heart burns with the question, just like the flame that burns the bush without consuming it. In the fire Moses hears his name. He knows that he is on holy ground.

At the foot of the mountain, before the burning bush, he opens himself to God's presence: "Here I am." In the moment of Moses's total surrender, God extends a total embrace. In that embrace Moses is welcomed home, a home that is at once God and, at the same moment, Moses. Encountering such love, Moses is overwhelmed. This showing forth of God's presence, his "face," is nearly too much for Moses.

# Suggested Approach to Prayer: Before the Burning Bush

## Daily Prayer Pattern
I quiet myself and relax in the presence of God.
I declare my dependence on God.

## Grace
I ask for the grace of freedom, for a readiness to respond with a clear yes to whatever I am called to by God.

## Method: Contemplation

I imagine myself as Moses. I allow the homelessness, the isolation that was his suffering, to become one with my own experience of being alone.

I become aware that my questions of identity and purpose are not unlike those of Moses.

I join with Moses in encountering the burning bush. I gaze into the fire. I visualize the brightness and feel the intense heat. I hear the crackling of the flames as they leap about the branches without consuming them.

Do I have within me the freedom to respond to God as Moses did, with "Here I am, Lord"?

I close my prayer with the Our Father.

## Review of Prayer

I write in my journal any feelings, experiences, or insights that have come to my awareness during this prayer period.

# Week Four, Day 3

# The Blessing of Trust

.........................................................................

### GENESIS 22:1–18

After these things God tested Abraham. He said to him, "Abraham!" And he said, "Here I am." He said, "Take your son, your only son Isaac, whom you love, and go to the land of Moriah, and offer him there as a burnt offering on one of the mountains that I shall show you."

So Abraham rose early in the morning, saddled his donkey, and took two of his young men with him, and his son Isaac; he cut the wood for the burnt offering, and set out and went to the place in the distance that God had shown him. On the third day Abraham looked up and saw the place far away. Then Abraham said to his young men, "Stay here with the donkey; the boy and I will go over there; we will worship, and then we will come back to you."

Abraham took the wood of the burnt offering and laid it on his son Isaac, and he himself carried the fire and the knife. So the two of them walked on together. Isaac said to his father Abraham, "Father!" And he said, "Here I am, my son." He said, "The fire and the wood are here, but where is the lamb for a burnt offering?" Abraham said, "God himself will provide the lamb for a burnt offering, my son." So the two of them walked on together.

When they came to the place that God had shown him, Abraham built an altar there and laid the wood in order. He bound his son Isaac, and laid him on the altar, on top of the wood. Then Abraham reached out his hand and took the knife to kill his son.

But the angel of the LORD called to him from heaven, and said, "Abraham, Abraham!" And he said, "Here I am." He said, "Do not lay your hand on the boy or do anything to him; for now I know that you fear God, since you have not withheld your son, your only son, from me." And Abraham looked up and saw a ram, caught in a thicket by its horns. Abraham went and took the ram and offered it up as a burnt offering instead of his son. So Abraham called that place "The LORD will provide"; as it is said to this day, "On the mount of the LORD it shall be provided."

The angel of the LORD called to Abraham a second time from heaven, and said, "By myself I have sworn, says the LORD: Because you have done this, and have not withheld your son, your only son, I will indeed bless you, and I will make your offspring as numerous as the stars of heaven and as the sand that is on the seashore. And your offspring shall possess the gate of their enemies, and by your offspring shall all the nations of the earth gain blessing for themselves, because you have obeyed my voice."

# Commentary

WE SEE A VERY OLD man laboriously walking up a mountain path. His eyes are taut with unshed tears and are fixed to the ground as if he does not dare look up. He carries a small black firebox that contains live coals, and in his belt is a knife.

Walking beside the man in silence is a young boy. On his shoulders he carries a heavy bundle of wood. The wood is so heavy and awkward that he walks unsteadily, almost losing his balance. On his face is an expression of confusion and fear. Every few steps he looks at his father in an attempt to discover why they are doing what they are doing. It is Abraham with his son Isaac.

Abraham and Sarah had given up hope of ever bearing a child, but through the mercy and goodness of God, the seemingly impossible happened. They conceived in their old age. Like other couples who give birth to a child in their later years, they experienced delight in their "late arrival."

There was an added dimension of joy for Abraham. In a special way, Isaac held for Abraham the promise of the future. He deeply believed that Isaac was meant by God to be the link, the continuation of what God had initiated in Abraham—that is, the creation of a people formed and bonded in God's love. Now God asks Abraham to kill his child.

Everything in Abraham questions this directive. His whole being reels under the impact of the paradox. God sent Isaac. Now he demands Isaac's death, and at the hand of Abraham.

Abraham is at a crossroads; he is facing the ultimate test. Does he have the courage to surrender to God's demand, to accept the dark unknowingly, and thereby let go of all his preconceived, rational assumptions?

This story is usually presented as an illustration of Abraham's obedience or as a statement against child sacrifice, which was common in the time of Abraham. However, the story of Abraham and Isaac is particularly significant in that it contains a profound personal experience that serves as a paradigm for the leap from the known to the unknown, the let-go experience that is at the heart of a mature knowledge and commitment to God.

The object of the story is not that God rushed in at the last moment to save Isaac and things returned to their previous status. No, everything changed. Abraham was different; Isaac was different. In yielding all, Abraham and Isaac set into motion the human journey toward holiness and wholeness in Christ!

As we look at Isaac, beloved by this father, struggling with the weight of the wood, can we see Jesus carrying the cross to Golgotha (John 19:17)?

# Suggested Approach to Prayer: Choice in Freedom

## Daily Prayer Pattern
I quiet myself and relax in the presence of God.
I declare my dependence on God.

## Grace
I ask for the grace of freedom, for a readiness to respond with a clear yes to whatever I am called to by God.

## Method: Contemplation
I imagine myself as Abraham responding to God's directive. I imagine the story in great detail, using all my senses to enter into the drama.

I am particularly aware of the inner turmoil at the moment of decision. What is my response? Am I able to surrender, in trust, to God's directive to me?

I close my prayer with the Our Father.

## Review of Prayer
I write in my journal any feelings, experiences, or insights that have come to my awareness during this prayer period.

Week Four, Day 4

# From Law to Love

.........................................................................................

## Philippians 3:7–11

Yet whatever gains I had, these I have come to regard as loss because of Christ. More than that, I regard everything as loss because of the surpassing value of knowing Christ Jesus my Lord. For his sake I have suffered the loss of all things, and I regard them as rubbish, in order that I may gain Christ and be found in him, not having a righteousness of my own that comes from the law, but one that comes through faith in Christ, the righteousness from God based on faith. I want to know Christ and the power of his resurrection and the sharing of his sufferings by becoming like him in his death, if somehow I may attain the resurrection from the dead.

## Commentary

BRING TO MIND AND HEART an intimately freeing relationship of love, such as one with your spouse or with a close friend. How did the relationship come about? What were the surprises? How would you describe your loved one? Are you satisfied to describe this person with factual information, such as the place and date of birth, or do you find yourself without adequate words to express what your heart knows of the other?

Our human experience of love is the context in which we discover how to love Christ. We experience deep levels of intimacy in our human relationships, and amazingly, we are offered the possibility of deep intimacy with Christ.

Just as our love relationship is a gift and never the result of our manipulative efforts, the love of Christ is always a gift. Through Paul's story, we are assured that in the acceptance of this intimate relationship of Christ's love, we will be released from any compulsiveness and rigidity that bind us. Fullness and wholeness come in the receiving of love offered. The degree to which we open ourselves to receive love corresponds to the degree to which we will experience our freedom.

In chapter 3 of his letter to the Philippians, Paul shares his personal relationship with Christ. All he wants to know is Christ, the power of his resurrection, and to share his life. He desires not to know *about* Christ but to *know* him personally. What we see in this passage is that Paul passed over from a relationship based on law to one founded on intimate love. He passed from legalism to freedom. In every authentic relationship there is this passage, this leap, to a new level of consciousness.

As we reflect on this letter of Paul, we become aware that our human experience of love can discover its full potential in the intimacy of union with Christ.

# Suggested Approach to Prayer: Dialogue with Christ

## Daily Prayer Pattern

I quiet myself and relax in the presence of God.
I declare my dependence on God.

## Grace

I ask for the grace of freedom, for a readiness to respond with a clear yes to whatever I am called to by God and a willingness to let go of all that is not in accordance with his values.

## Method: Journaling

(It will be helpful to read about journaling on pages 7 and 8)

I write a conversation between myself and Jesus. I express fully my most profound sense of him.

I write his responses to me, allowing his Spirit to address me through the written word.

I close my prayer with the Our Father.

## Review of Prayer

I write in my journal any feelings, experiences, or insights that have come to my awareness during this prayer period.

# Week Four, Day 5

# Hope

.....................................................................................

## ROMANS 8:18-25

I consider that the sufferings of this present time are not worth comparing with the glory about to be revealed to us. For the creation waits with eager longing for the revealing of the children of God; for the creation was subjected to futility, not of its own will but by the will of the one who subjected it, in hope that the creation itself will be set free from its bondage to decay and will obtain the freedom of the glory of the children of God. We know that the whole creation has been groaning in labor pains until now; and not only the creation, but we ourselves, who have the first fruits of the Spirit, groan inwardly while we wait for adoption, the redemption of our bodies. For in hope we were saved. Now hope that is seen is not hope. For who hopes for what is seen? But if we hope for what we do not see, we wait for it with patience.

## Commentary

JUST WHEN WE THINK THE end is upon us, we discover it is the beginning! Just when we think our children are totally lost to us, we realize they are crossing over into adulthood. Just when we think a friendship has totally collapsed, we become aware that it is being transformed from one of dependent need to one of mutual joy. Just when we think a parish or congregation has become irrevocably fragmented, we see bursting forth a community based on authentic participatory leadership. Just when we think that widespread violence and terrorism will destroy civilization, we witness a rising swell of compassion. To be alive is to be in transition. It is to enter into the passages that mark our growth and development as mature men and women in Christ.

We know that the whole creation has been groaning in labor pains until now—and not only the creation, but we ourselves. God presents us with challenges that demand all that we are and bless us with more than we dare dream. We are challenged to be patient and to realize that, within our own time and space, we are, though broken and limited, moving toward the creation of a new age. We and all of creation are being thrust forward into the freedom and glory of new life in Christ.

We are challenged to suffer while holding on to the belief that suffering is a vital part of the transition toward new life. We are challenged to eagerly expect that the workings of the Holy Spirit, though often hidden, will be unleashed and made visible. In the chaos of our lives, Paul—and Jesus—call us to hope. In hope is our freedom.

# Suggested Approach to Prayer: Prayer of Healing

## Daily Prayer Pattern

I quiet myself and relax in the presence of God.
I declare my dependence on God.

## Grace

I ask for the grace of freedom, for a readiness to respond with a clear yes to whatever I am called to by God.

## Method: Meditation

I identify my deepest suffering or lack of peace at this time in my life.

I listen to my wise mentor, Paul, speak his words to me in the words of the passage. As he speaks to me, I relate his words to my suffering. I listen deeply and open my pain to receive the healing energy of God's creative, hope-filled love.

I close my prayer with the Our Father.

## Review of Prayer

I write in my journal any feelings, experiences, or insights that have come to my awareness during this prayer period.

Week Four, Day 6

# Repetition

## Suggested Approach to Prayer

### Daily Prayer Pattern

I quiet myself and relax in the presence of God.

I declare my dependence on God.

### Grace

I ask for the grace of freedom, for a readiness to respond with a clear yes to whatever I am called to by God.

### Method: Repetition

In preparation, I review my prayer by reading my journal of the past week. I select for my repetition the period of prayer in which I was most deeply moved by joy, gratitude, or awe, or perhaps a passage that did not seem to touch me at all, or only painfully so. I proceed in the manner I did originally, opening my heart to this word of God.

### Review of Prayer

I write in my journal any feelings, experiences, or insights that have come to my awareness during this prayer period. I am particularly aware of how God may be giving me the grace I have been requesting.

## Week Five, Day 1

# Within the Chaos

............................................................................................

### Isaiah 45:9–13 (Jerusalem Bible)

Can it argue with the man who fashioned it,
One vessel among earthen vessels?
Does the clay say to its fashioner, "What are you making?"
does the thing he shaped say, "You have no skill"?
Woe to him who says to a father, "What have you begotten?"
or to a woman, "To what have you given birth?"

Thus says Yahweh,
the Holy One, he who fashions Israel:
Is it for you to question me about my children
and to dictate to me what my hands should do?
I it was who made the earth,
and created man who is on it.
I it was who spread out the heavens with my hands
And now give orders to their whole array.
I it was who roused him to victory.
I leveled the way for him.
He will rebuild my city,
will bring my exiles back
without ransom or indemnity,
so says Yahweh Sabaoth.

# Commentary

PRIMITIVE PEOPLE RECOGNIZED GOD IN nature, not only in the tranquility and beauty but more dramatically in the unleashed power of wind, flood, and fire. Just as God is present in nature, he is present within our history. It seems, however, much easier to be in touch with the God of nature because being in touch with the God of history requires reflection and a historical perspective. No less dramatic than in nature are the forces and energies unleashed within human history. To "read" God's word in history demands a deep faith that God is present and active in the human situation.

This passage from the book of Isaiah alerts us to how necessary it is to reflect upon and become astute at recognizing God's activity within world circumstances and historical events. The historical circumstance emphasized in this passage is God's action in the appointment of Cyrus. Incredibly, Cyrus, a pagan, is an instrument of God in bringing about the reestablishment of Israel at the end of a long period of exile. For the Hebrew people, the passage helped them recall God's faithfulness in the past and sustain their confidence for the future.

Unlike most cultures, the Hebrew people had an innate grasp of how God had been present to them within their history. This came primarily from a vivid recollection of their deliverance from Egyptian slavery. They knew by faith that God had directly intervened and led them to freedom across the Red Sea (also known as the Reed Sea because of the reeds growing along it).

In Yahweh, the God of history and the God of nature converged. The Hebrew people discovered that the God of history who delivered them was also the God of nature who forged them creatively into a chosen people, a consecrated nation.

Our freedom is contingent on our degree of trust that God is just as present within the chaos—the fire, flood, and wind—of contemporary events as he was present for the Hebrew people of ancient times. We, too, are to maintain confidence in him. To surrender to his saving presence is to participate in the unfolding of his continuing creation.

# Suggested Approach to Prayer: Praying over Our Times

## Daily Prayer Pattern

I quiet myself and relax in the presence of God.
I declare my dependence on God.

## Grace

I ask for the grace of freedom, for a readiness to see God's presence alive in our world.

## Method

I prayerfully read the passage, letting the words find a home in me.

I quietly page through a news magazine or newspaper. I read the headlines and look at the pictures with the eyes of faith. I intersperse my reflective perusal of the magazine or newspaper with a preferred line from the Scripture passage, such as "I made the earth" or "He will rebuild my city."

I close my prayer with the Our Father.

## Review of Prayer

I write in my journal any feelings, experiences, or insights that have come to my awareness during this prayer period.

## Week Five, Day 2

# Faith

......................................................................

### Hebrews 11:17–19

By faith Abraham, when put to the test, offered up Isaac. He who had received the promises was ready to offer up his only son, of whom he had been told, "It is through Isaac that descendants shall be named for you." He considered the fact that God is able even to raise someone from the dead—and figuratively speaking, he did receive him back.

## Commentary

Have you ever sensed that in some circumstance facing you, everything seemed to fit together? Perhaps the project or task before you was to build a home, begin a new career, return to school, or write a book. The time was ripe. The direction seemed so clear that within yourself you experienced it as God's intention for you. You claimed the task. You embraced the direction so deeply that it became for you the external expression of your personal relationship with God and his action through you.

You began. Obstacles arose; doors seemed to close. Tuition was more expensive than you imagined; career options were limited; there did not seem to be any interest in the subject you had chosen to write about! But in spite of the impediments, you continued to move ahead. You may have pulled back a bit, or slowed down, but you continued to plan and to work toward your goal.

You persevered because you believed in your dream. You believed that within yourself you had the gifts necessary. You believed that what you were doing would contribute significantly to something or someone beyond yourself. In the face of the obstacles, you did not understand how this was going to be accomplished. It was not clear, but you went ahead.

This is faith. *Faith* is an abstract word that, like love, has been overused to the point of having little content. For many people, faith is reduced to intellectual assent; for them faith never makes the journey from the head to the heart. Authentic faith resides most deeply in the heart.

One of the examples of faith held up by the author of Hebrews is Abraham's faith as expressed in his obedience to God when the death of his only son Isaac was demanded. Abraham did not comprehend why God would take away the life of the person upon whom rested the promise of the future of the Israelites. It did not make any sense! Yet Abraham believed. His belief plunged him into the forces of darkness and death, which, paradoxically, issued forth in new life.

Some things are constant: faith for us is what faith was for Abraham. We, too, have our "Isaacs," those things or persons given to us that we see as means to some ultimate fulfillment. Only when we surrender them to God can they become sources of life and grace. In the deliverance of Isaac, we find a symbol of the mystery of the death and resurrection of Jesus.

# Suggested Approach to Prayer: Meeting Isaac

## Daily Prayer Pattern

I quiet myself and relax in the presence of God.
I declare my dependence on God.

## Grace

I ask for the gift of freedom, a readiness to respond with a clear "yes" to whatever I am called to by God.

## Method: Meditation

I ponder: What is it that is most precious in my life? A child? A career? A dream? My health?

I see it before me as Abraham saw and embraced Isaac.

What is the worst thing that could happen?

I speak to God about my "Isaac." I tell him what it means to me. I listen to hear what God will say to me about what it means to him, and what I mean to him.

If I am able, I offer my Isaac to God; I receive Isaac back from God.

If I am not able to offer my Isaac, I humbly beg for the desire.

I close my prayer with the Our Father.

## Review of Prayer

I write in my journal any feelings, experiences, or insights that have come to my awareness during this prayer period.

# Week Five, Day 3
# Side by Side

·········································································································

### 1 CORINTHIANS 9:19–23

For though I am free with respect to all, I have made myself a slave to all, so that I might win more of them. To the Jews I became as a Jew, in order to win Jews. To those under the law I became as one under the law (though I myself am not under the law) so that I might win those under the law. To those outside the law I became as one outside the law (though I am not free from God's law but am under Christ's law) so that I might win those outside the law. To the weak I became weak, so that I might win the weak. I have become all things to all people, so that I might by any means save some. I do it all for the sake of the gospel, so that I may share in its blessings.

## Commentary

"SIDE BY SIDE"—THIS PHRASE APTLY describes Paul's way of sharing God's love. He becomes, as he said, all things to all people.

This saying is often negated by the seemingly impossible demands it makes; it causes people to react with, "Well, one can't be all things to all people." This frequently results in a rationalization for not being anything to anyone. Paul is not suggesting that we do all things for all people. We are never to assume the responsibility for others.

Rather, he is speaking of his own attitude of adapting himself to the situation of others. This attitude flows from Paul's deep conviction that Christ reveals himself to each person within each one's particular circumstances.

Christ had grasped Paul so profoundly that he was able to become confident and free enough to let go of the rigidities of Jewish religious law. No longer did the laws bind or control Paul; in the love of Christ he discovered their deeper meaning.

The original intent of the law was to serve the people, but it had become an absolute value unto itself. For Paul, the absolute value within the law would always be the love of Christ.

The ultimate worth of any value—whether personal, national, or legal—is determined and judged by how well it serves and promotes the law of love. Being free in the law, Paul became a servant of love. He was able to communicate to those still bound by legalism as well as those who rejected any law at all. His own freedom allowed him to move with ease and to accommodate the message to whomever he was addressing.

This "side by side" ministry serves as an example for our ministry of love. What was required of Paul is required of us as well. Like Paul, we are to open ourselves to receive the love of God and to receive, within that love, all others.

Paul's voluntary submission to others, his "slavery," reflects the spirit of his master, Jesus, who emptied himself, taking the form of a slave (Philippians 2:7).

# Suggested Approach to Prayer: The Eyes of Jesus

### Daily Prayer Pattern

I quiet myself and relax in the presence of God.
I declare my dependence on God.

## Grace

I ask for the grace of a radical openness before God.

## Method: Centering Prayer (refer to page 5)

I see Jesus before me, looking at me.

I allow him to look at me lovingly and humbly.

I realize that Jesus, in becoming human, became a servant of love.

I open myself to receive his attention and care.

I close my prayer with the Our Father.

## Review of Prayer

I write in my journal any feelings, experiences, or insights that have come to my awareness during this prayer period.

Week Five, Day 4

# In Christ

······································································································

## PHILIPPIANS 1:21–26

For to me, living is Christ and dying is gain. If I am to live in the flesh, that means fruitful labor for me; and I do not know which I prefer. I am hard pressed between the two: my desire is to depart and be with Christ, for that is far better; but to remain in the flesh is more necessary for you. Since I am convinced of this, I know that I will remain and continue with all of you for your progress and joy in faith, so that I may share abundantly in your boasting in Christ Jesus when I come to you again.

## Commentary

PAUL WROTE HIS BEAUTIFUL AND loving letter to the people of Philippi from his prison cell. For Paul, as for anyone, to be in prison was to face the issue of his own death; imprisonment was in fact an ancient symbol for death. The prison cell frequently was a windowless room with an opening in the ceiling through which the prisoner was dropped. It was the nearest thing to a tomb that one could imagine. Here Paul awaited the trial that he knew was likely to result in his death.

This letter bears the contemplative quality of one who had entered into his deepest self and found Christ. In himself, Paul wrestled with the contradictions of life. For Paul, to continue to live was, in a sense, to die—that is, to delay his complete union with Christ. In contrast, for him to die would be ultimate life in that he would at last arrive at total unity with Christ. He is in the dilemma between his own desires and the needs of those he loves and wants to bring to Christ. The weight is on the side of those he loves.

In the surrender of his own desire, as he places the matter of his life or death into the hands of God, Paul discovers the freedom of profound indifference. What previously appeared contradictory is now resolved in the acceptance of paradox. Love has revealed this resolution and led the way to it.

Paul arrives at the realization that to die or not to die is really not the question. The point of the entire argument is to be in Christ. Although there surely is some advantage in death, he knows that being with and forming the Christian community is no less a union with Christ.

This beautiful prayer, traditionally attributed to St. Patrick, might well be Paul's:

Christ within me, Christ before me, Christ behind me,
Christ in me, Christ beneath me, Christ above me,
Christ on my right, Christ on my left,
Christ when I lie down, Christ when I sit down, Christ when I arise,
Christ in the heart of every one who thinks of me,
Christ in the mouth of every one who speaks of me,
Christ in every eye that sees me,
Christ in every ear that hears me.

# Suggested Approach to Prayer: Descent into Prison

## Daily Prayer Pattern

I quiet myself and relax in the presence of God.
I declare my dependence on God.

## Grace

I ask for the grace of radical openness before God.

## Method: Contemplation

I imagine myself being lowered into the prison with Paul. As I am lowered, I experience the depth of this prison. I gradually become aware of the darkness and the damp cold. My feelings descend upon me, feelings of aloneness and fear.

I am aware that I am being chained. What are these chains? What are the contradictions that are holding me bound and imprisoned?

Are they anxieties about a long or short life, about health or sickness, riches or poverty, honor or dishonor?

I invite Jesus to be the resolution of whatever life dilemma I am presently experiencing.

I close my prayer by slowly praying the prayer of St. Patrick.

## Review of Prayer

I write in my journal any feelings, experiences, or insights that have come to my awareness during this prayer period.

## Week Five, Day 5

# Repetition

..................................................................................

## Suggested Approach to Prayer

### Daily Prayer Pattern

I quiet myself and relax in the presence of God.
I declare my dependence on God.

### Grace

I ask God for the grace of a radical openness before God.

### Method: Repetition

In preparation, I review my prayer by reading my journal of the past week. I select for my repetition the period of prayer in which I was most deeply moved by joy, gratitude, or awe, or perhaps a passage that did not seem to speak to me at all, or only painfully so. I proceed in the manner suggested for the passage, opening my heart to hear the unique meaning of the word of God for me.

### Review of Prayer

I write in my journal any feelings, experiences, or insights that have come to my awareness during this prayer period. I am particularly aware of how God may be giving me the grace I have been requesting.

Week Five, Day 6

# The Bridegroom

.............................................................................................

## JOHN 3:22–32

After this Jesus and his disciples went into the Judean countryside, and he spent some time there with them and baptized. John also was baptizing at Aenon near Salim because water was abundant there; and people kept coming and were being baptized—John, of course, had not yet been thrown into prison.

Now a discussion about purification arose between John's disciples and a Jew. They came to John and said to him, "Rabbi, the one who was with you across the Jordan, to whom you testified, here he is baptizing, and all are going to him." John answered, "No one can receive anything except what has been given from heaven. You yourselves are my witnesses that I said, 'I am not the Messiah, but I have been sent ahead of him.' He who has the bride is the bridegroom. The friend of the bridegroom, who stands and hears him, rejoices greatly at the bridegroom's voice. For this reason my joy has been fulfilled. He must increase, but I must decrease."

The one who comes from above is above all; the one who is of the earth belongs to the earth and speaks about earthly things. The one who comes from heaven is above all. He testifies to what he has seen and heard, yet no one accepts his testimony.

## Commentary

ALL ARE GOING TO HIM (verse 26). This verse gives focus to the passage, which becomes clear as it unfolds. The people are going to "him." They are drawn like moths to light, like those who thirst are drawn to the spring. The one they are drawn to is Jesus! He is the bridegroom!

The relationship between Jesus and John the Baptist receives beautiful expression in the rich imagery of eastern wedding customs. The use of marriage imagery recalls the covenant relationship between God and Israel, which was so close a bond that only the intimate union of marriage could begin to express it. In the Old Testament, God is represented as a bridegroom and Israel is the bride. In the New Testament, Jesus is the bridegroom, the church is the bride, and John sees himself in the role of best man. Under the canopy of Old Testament imagery, each takes his or her proper role as God has ordained it. Jesus is the bridegroom. He is the central figure toward whom everyone gravitates. He is not only the central figure of the New Testament, but he holds within his person, and is representative of, the collective consciousness of the entire people of Israel.

To understand John's role, it is helpful to understand the role of best man in Jewish custom. As is customary even today, the man who is chosen as best man is usually the groom's best friend. In the time of Jesus, the honor of being chosen as best man was even more distinctive. He was the one in charge of arranging for the wedding, and he presided as host at the feast. However, his most important responsibility was that of guarding the bridal chamber until the groom joined the bride. Only then were his duties completed.

John's task was to bring together Jesus and the community that John himself had nurtured and prepared for this moment. This is the same role Moses had with respect to the Old Testament covenant between God and Israel. John, however, has even greater cause for joy and celebration. What Moses prophesied and foreshadowed has, through God's great love, been fulfilled. In Jesus, God has definitively embraced his people.

Having completed his task of preparing the way for Jesus, John withdraws. He willingly, even joyfully, directs the attention away from himself to Jesus. To anyone who would ask, John's reply might well have been:

> I listen; he is the one that speaks;
>
> I am enlightened; he is the light;
>
> "I am the ear; he is the word." (St. Augustine)
>
> I am the best man; Jesus is the bridegroom, and now is my "joy . . . fulfilled".

# Suggested Approach to Prayer: In His Light

## Daily Prayer Pattern

I quiet myself and relax in the presence of God.

I declare my dependence on God.

## Grace

I ask for the grace to desire to know and do God's will, to commit myself to what is more for the greater honor and glory of God.

## Method: Centering Prayer

I see myself as a candle flame burning brightly. I have been burning for a long time, and my flame is strong and casts a warm, beautiful glow.

Suddenly a brilliant light appears as if from a lighthouse. The light permeates and warms the entire space, spreading intense brightness.

I feel myself being absorbed by the light. My own flame seems to grow smaller and smaller until it is barely visible.

I relax in the glow; I allow myself to be embraced and held in its radiance.

I focus my heart on Jesus as light, and very quietly repeat the name of Jesus.

I close my prayer with the Our Father.

## Review of Prayer

I write in my journal any feelings, experiences, or insights that have come to my awareness during this prayer period.

## Part Five

# Commitment

# Week Six, Day 1

# Here I Am

.................................................................................

### 1 SAMUEL 3:1–11

Now the boy Samuel was ministering to the LORD under Eli. The word of the LORD was rare in those days; visions were not widespread.

At that time Eli, whose eyesight had begun to grow dim so that he could not see, was lying down in his room; the lamp of God had not yet gone out, and Samuel was lying down in the temple of the LORD, where the ark of God was. Then the LORD called, "Samuel! Samuel!" and he said, "Here I am!" and ran to Eli, and said, "Here I am, for you called me." But he said, "I did not call; lie down again." So he went and lay down. The LORD called again, "Samuel!" Samuel got up and went to Eli, and said, "Here I am, for you called me." But he said, "I did not call, my son; lie down again." Now Samuel did not yet know the LORD, and the word of the LORD had not yet been revealed to him. The LORD called Samuel again, a third time. And he got up and went to Eli, and said, "Here I am, for you called me." Then Eli perceived that the LORD was calling the boy. Therefore Eli said to Samuel, "Go, lie down; and if he calls you, you shall say, 'Speak, LORD, for your servant is listening.'" So Samuel went and lay down in his place.

Now the LORD came and stood there, calling as before, "Samuel! Samuel!" And Samuel said, "Speak, for your servant is listening." Then the LORD said to Samuel, "See, I am about to do something in Israel that will make both ears of anyone who hears of it tingle."

# Commentary

GOD SPEAKS SOMETIMES IN THE gentle breeze, sometimes in the quiet of night, sometimes to that place in our hearts that is still childlike. In prayer, we hear our name called. This was Samuel's experience, just as it was the experience of the prophets who preceded him—Abraham, Jacob, and Moses. Samuel responded with the same words and the same total generosity and openness: "Here I am, Lord."

Each of us has an inner voice that calls us to be who we are. To be who we are is an "election" by God. To embrace the unique "word" God speaks in creating us, in calling us by name, is to encounter God.

To say, "Here I am, Lord," is to have the audacity to believe in, and the courage to exercise, the particular gifts that identify one's deepest self. One of the greatest temptations is to doubt our own experience of God. Eventually, we too may need an Eli—a representative of the community—with whom to test the spirit. Meanwhile, we, like Samuel, need to enter the night, rest, and listen for the moment when God speaks our name.

# Suggested Approach to Prayer: God Speaks My Name

## Daily Prayer Pattern

I quiet myself and relax in the presence of God.
I declare my dependence on God.

## Grace

I ask for the grace to desire to know and do God's will, and to commit myself to what is more for the greater glory and honor of God.

## Method: Contemplation

I enter into a state of profound relaxation, nearly asleep. As Samuel did, I hear God speak my name.

By what name does God call me? My full baptismal name? My nickname? A term of endearment? Or something else?

What is the tenor of God's voice as he speaks my name? Is it urgent? Gentle? Begging?

I open myself to receive his call.

I let my heart respond.

I close my prayer with the Our Father.

## Review of Prayer

I write in my journal any feelings, experiences, or insights that have come to my awareness during this prayer period.

## Week Six, Day 2

# Model for Surrender

................................................................................

### LUKE 1:26–38

In the sixth month the angel Gabriel was sent by God to a town
in Galilee called Nazareth, to a virgin engaged to a man whose
name was Joseph, of the house of David. The virgin's name was
Mary. And he came to her and said, "Greetings, favored one! The
Lord is with you." But she was much perplexed by his words and
pondered what sort of greeting this might be. The angel said to
her, "Do not be afraid, Mary, for you have found favor with God.
And now, you will conceive in your womb and bear a son, and
you will name him Jesus. He will be great, and will be called the
Son of the Most High, and the Lord God will give to him the
throne of his ancestor David. He will reign over the house of
Jacob forever, and of his kingdom there will be no end." Mary said
to the angel, "How can this be, since I am a virgin?" The angel said
to her, "The Holy Spirit will come upon you, and the power of the
Most High will overshadow you; therefore the child to be born
will be holy; he will be called Son of God. And now, your relative
Elizabeth in her old age has also conceived a son; and this is the
sixth month for her who was said to be barren. For nothing will
be impossible with God." Then Mary said, "Here am I, the servant
of the Lord; let it be with me according to your word." Then the
angel departed from her.

## Commentary

"LET IT BE WITH ME according to your word." This response of Mary to the angelic announcement of the birth of Jesus reveals Mary to us as the first Christian disciple.

Some scholars suggest that, in writing this passage, Luke drew on what he knew of Mary in her later ministry. We know that Jesus praised his mother as one of those who heard the word of God and put it into practice (Luke 8:21). She was a woman obedient to the word of God.

At the moment of Mary's willing response to God's action in her life, all the hopes of humanity were realized. She is the convergent point of the two covenants. In her, the covenant of God with Israel gave way to the emergence of the covenant of Christ with his church. Mary is, therefore, the mother of the church. The Word of God was conceived within her, and in the Word all things are conceived.

What every follower of Jesus is called to do, Mary did first. She exemplified what we read in John 12:24: Unless a grain of wheat falls into the earth and dies, it remains just a single grain; but if it dies, it bears much fruit.

In Mary's total yielding of self, we recognize the same spirit of total surrender to the Father that characterized the final cry of her Son: Into your hands I commend my spirit (Luke 23:46).

## Suggested Approach to Prayer: With Mary

### Daily Prayer Pattern

I quiet myself and relax in the presence of God.

I declare my dependence on God.

# Grace

I ask for the grace to desire to know and to do God's will, and to commit myself to what is more for the glory of God.

# Method: Contemplation

I imagine myself as Mary. I use the passage as a script to enter into the unfolding drama of the annunciation.

I picture myself in the home of Mary, suddenly startled by the visit of an angel.

I allow myself to be opened to her experience of surprise, fear, confusion, amazement, and ultimately, to her generosity of response.

With Mary, I yield to God's inviting word and spirit within my heart.

I close my prayer with the Our Father.

# Review of Prayer

I write in my journal any feelings, experiences, or insights that have come to my awareness during this prayer period.

# Week Six, Day 3
# Plea for Wisdom

......................................................................................

## WISDOM 9:1–12

O God of my ancestors and Lord of mercy,
who have made all things by your word,
and by your wisdom have formed humankind
to have dominion over the creatures you have made,
and rule the world in holiness and righteousness,
and pronounce judgment in uprightness of soul,
give me the wisdom that sits by your throne,
and do not reject me from among your servants.
For I am your servant the son of your serving girl,
a man who is weak and short-lived,
with little understanding of judgment and laws;
for even one who is perfect among human beings
will be regarded as nothing without the wisdom that comes from you.
You have chosen me to be king of your people
and to be judge over your sons and daughters.
You have given command to build a temple on your holy mountain,
and an altar in the city of your habitation,
a copy of the holy tent that you prepared from the beginning.
With you is wisdom, she who knows your works
and was present when you made the world;
she understands what is pleasing in your sight
and what is right according to your commandments.

Send her forth from the holy heavens, and from the throne of your
>    glory send her,
that she may labor at my side,
and that I may learn what is pleasing to you.
For she knows and understands all things,
and she will guide me wisely in my actions
and guard me with her glory.
Then my works will be acceptable,
and I shall judge your people justly,
and shall be worthy of the throne of my father.

# Commentary

SHE HASTENS TO MAKE HERSELF known to those who desire her
(Wisdom 6:13). When she is your friend, all good things will
come to you (7:11). Her radiance never ceases (7:10). She will be
for you an unfailing treasure, and through her you will become
friends with God (7:14). She is a beautiful woman (Proverbs 8:1–
21) and mirrors God's own goodness (Wisdom 7:26). She will be
your comfort and your counselor (8:9). Pray, and she will come
to you (7:7).

Her name is Wisdom.

In Old Testament wisdom literature, wisdom is represented as a woman. As the feminine dimension of God's power,
wisdom is seen as accompanying the Lord in his creation
(Proverbs 8:22–31).

To receive the gift of wisdom from God is to have the knowledge and skill to respond with ease to life situations and prob-
lems. Wisdom enables us to encounter life with a balanced
framework and in a realistic, practical, and moral manner.

Through this gift of discernment, we become partners with God in his ongoing creation.

Wisdom 9:1–12 is a prayer, placed on the lips of the king, who asks for wisdom.

# Suggested Approach to Prayer: To Speak with Wisdom

## Daily Prayer Pattern

I quiet myself and relax in the presence of God.
I declare my dependence on God.

## Grace

I ask for the gift that all my desires will be ordered to the fulfillment of God's plan and wisdom.

## Method: Journaling

I see Wisdom as a person. I imagine her. What does she look like? Old or young? How is she dressed? What do I know of her? Where does she live? How far has she traveled? What are her experiences? What has been my relationship with her, now and in the past?

I enter into a written conversation with Wisdom. She speaks to me; I respond to her. I relax and let the words flow freely from my pen.

I reverently reread the passage.

I conclude my prayer with the Our Father.

# Review of Prayer

I write in my journal any feelings, experiences, or insights that have come to my awareness during this prayer period.

## Week Six, Day 4

# From Judge to Lover

............................................................................

## ROMANS 8:31–39

What then are we to say about these things? If God is for us, who is against us? He who did not withhold his own Son, but gave him up for all of us, will he not with him also give us everything else? Who will bring any charge against God's elect? It is God who justifies. Who is to condemn? It is Christ Jesus, who died, yes, who was raised, who is at the right hand of God, who indeed intercedes for us.

Who will separate us from the love of Christ? Will hardship, or distress, or persecution, or famine, or nakedness, or peril, or sword? As it is written, "For your sake we are being killed all day long; we are accounted as sheep to be slaughtered." No, in all these things we are more than conquerors through him who loved us.

For I am convinced that neither death, nor life, nor angels, nor rulers, nor things present, nor things to come, nor powers, nor height, nor depth, nor anything else in all creation, will be able to separate us from the love of God in Christ Jesus our Lord.

## Commentary

"WE, THE JURY, FIND THE defendant not guilty as charged." This courtroom acquittal precipitates immense relief and joy for those who have been brought to the court of justice. With these words, one has been found innocent—and has been freed.

Our hearts, too, can rejoice! Our "judgment" has already taken place. We have been pronounced not guilty. We have been found innocent, and we are set free. This amazing announcement is the underlying conviction of the hymn of love found in Paul's letter to the Romans.

The significance of the passage lies in its being the bridge for us from our image of Christ as judge to one of Christ as lover. In verses 31–35, we are assured that God is on our side and has acquitted us. Can anyone condemn us? If anyone could, or would have the right, it would be Jesus. Jesus knows how much we sin because by his sufferings he has taken our faults on himself.

However, Jesus does not act as our judge. Although Jesus pleads our cause, it is not as a trial attorney but rather out of deep love. He stands as the one who will be heard, at the Father's right hand, appealing to God to grant us innocence—that is, freedom. It is the freedom to love and to receive love. In Jesus, God's love is translated into human terms. He is the image of the invisible God, the firstborn of all creation (Colossians 1:15).

God has thought of us and loved us just as he has thought of and loved his Son. We, too, have been created in his image (Genesis 1:27). We are sons and daughters of God, and as such are to respond to God with love, the love that originated with God, for he first loved us (1 John 4:19). In other words, the love originates in God. It is the essence, the very breath of our existence. Therefore, we cannot possibly be separated from love, from God.

Our union with Jesus expresses the fullness of that love. Temptation or suffering cannot rob us of it but can only draw us deeper into love. In some mysterious way, our sufferings and temptations, even though hidden, are part of Jesus' own suffering and temptation.

We are loved! Can he who did not spare his own Son for our sake refuse us anything?

# Suggested Approach to Prayer: Conversation with Jesus

## Daily Prayer Pattern

I quiet myself and relax in the presence of God.
I declare my dependence on God.

## Grace

I ask for the gift of experiencing deeply the love of Jesus for me.

## Method: Contemplation

I imagine Jesus sitting close to me. He is present to me as a friend who loves me.

I speak to him. I tell him of my deepest desires, greatest joys, and most profound fears.

If there is no one else around, I speak aloud.

I listen to what he says to me; I pause frequently to listen to what Jesus wishes to express to me in my heart.

As the conversation concludes, I repeat the name of Jesus over and over, slowly and quietly.

I pray the Our Father with Jesus.

## Review of Prayer

I write in my journal any feelings, experiences, or insights that have come to my awareness during this prayer period.

## Week Six, Day 5

# Christ: Fullness of God

......................................................................................

### EPHESIANS 3:14–21

For this reason I bow my knees before the Father, from whom
every family in heaven and on earth takes its name. I pray that,
according to the riches of his glory, he may grant that you may be
strengthened in your inner being with power through his Spirit, and
that Christ may dwell in your hearts through faith, as you are being
rooted and grounded in love. I pray that you may have the power
to comprehend, with all the saints, what is the breadth and length
and height and depth, and to know the love of Christ that surpasses
knowledge, so that you may be filled with all the fullness of God.

Now to him who by the power at work within us is able to
accomplish abundantly far more than all we can ask or imagine, to
him be glory in the church and in Christ Jesus to all generations,
forever and ever. Amen.

## Commentary

DO YOU REMEMBER EVER HAPPENING upon your mother or
father while they were at prayer? You may have become aware of
a quiet gentleness of expression, or even tears. It was as if you had
entered a hidden, sacred space.

Reading this passage is somewhat like coming upon Paul
while he is at prayer. He reveals to us his deep love of Christ and
his concern for the church. His own personal struggle is also
reflected in his prayer.

Paul is kneeling; Jews usually stood to pray. To kneel while praying was more characteristic of pagans. Paul may have assumed this form as a way of expressing his hope for the eventual union of Jews and Gentiles. It may well have been an ecumenical gesture. Or it may simply have been, for him, a spontaneous act precipitated by the intensity of his prayer.

In the prayer, Paul places himself before the Father. The intimate tone of the passage tells us something of Paul's relationship with God; it was as a son to his father. With the birth of Christianity, the fatherhood of God came to be seen as offering total accessibility and intimacy to all.

Paul's prayer is a prayer for oneness with Christ. His world was much like our own; it was an age of transition characterized by the death of the old and the not-yet-realized birth of the new. Many of the systems—political, social, economic, and religious—were no longer viable or effective. It was a scenario of collapse and chaos.

Then, as now, what was occurring in the larger world was also taking place in individuals. As they struggled with the chaos that existed in themselves, they wrestled with the questions, Who am I? Am I a broken person in a broken world? and Where is my hope?

Paul knew brokenness. He was no stranger to inner struggles. Under the impact of his meeting with Christ on the road to Damascus (Acts 9), he experienced the collapse of his worldview, his personal identity, and his beliefs.

Paul also knew hope. He discovered that the "fullness of God" in Christ was what gave his life meaning. That is why he prays so fervently that the "hidden self" of his disciples would grow strong in, with, and through Christ.

Paul closes his prayer with praise to God for the transforming power that is his gift to all who believe in Jesus. It is through
this energizing Spirit of love that Jesus unites his followers, however diverse or estranged, and brings to fulfillment his presence
in his body, the church.

# Suggested Approach to Prayer: Praying with Paul

## Daily Prayer Pattern

I quiet myself and relax in the presence of God.
I declare my dependence on God.

## Grace

I ask for the grace to open my heart and receive God's love
deeply, with trust.

## Method: Meditation

I let my heart pray this passage for my deepest self. It is Paul's
prayer for me; it is the desire that Christ has for me. I let my heart
respond.

I will repeat reflectively the phrase that I find speaks most
directly to where I experience need.

I will pause and savor those phrases that I find most consol-
ing and most encouraging.

I close my prayer with the Our Father.

## Review of Prayer

I write in my journal any feelings, experiences, or insights that
have come to my awareness during this prayer period.

Week Six, Day 6

# Letter to God

## Suggested Approach to Prayer

### Daily Prayer Pattern

I quiet myself and relax in the presence of God.

I declare my dependence on God.

### Grace

I ask for the grace of profound thankfulness for the gift of God's love.

### Method: Repetition and Journaling

During several prayer periods, I reread my prayer journal of the past weeks. I become aware of how my prayer and the events of my life have mutually influenced each other during this time.

I recognize how God has spoken to me, in love, during these past weeks.

I use a prayer period to respond to his love by writing a letter to God. I let my heart speak.

# Appendix A:
# For Spiritual Directors

The passages and commentaries are keyed to the basic movements of the Principle and Foundation as it is found in the Spiritual Exercises of St. Ignatius.

## God's Love
Psalm 139:1–18

Isaiah 43:1–7

I John 4:7–8, 18–19

Exodus 19:3–4

Psalm 103

## God's Goodness
Hosea 11:1–9

Luke 12:4–7

Isaiah 49:14–16

Psalm 136

Psalm 8

## God's Creation
Jeremiah 18:1–6

Job 1:20–21

Psalm 104

Psalm 19

Job 38-39

## Spiritual Freedom/Indifference

Romans 9:20–21

Exodus 3:1–6

Genesis 22:1–18

Philippians 3:7–11

Romans 8:18–25

Isaiah 45:9–13

Hebrews 11:17–19

1 Corinthians 9:19–23

Philippians 1:21–26

## Commitment

John 3:22–32

1 Samuel 3:1–11

Luke 1:26–38

Wisdom 9:1–12

Romans 8:31–39

Ephesians 3:14–21

# Appendix B:
# Index of Approaches to Prayer

## God's Love:

Psalm 139:1–18: God in My Life (reflective exercise)

Isaiah 43:1–7: A Love Letter from God (meditation)

I John 4:7–8, 18–19: A Window on God (reflective meditation)

Exodus 19:3–4: An Astonishing Offer (meditation)

Psalm 103: The Energy of Love (meditation)

## God's Goodness:

Hosea 11:1–9: Loved and Forgiven (contemplation)

Luke 12:4–7: A Letter of Encouragement (meditation)

Isaiah 49:14–16: A Child Is Born (contemplation)

Psalm 136: His Steadfast Love (prayer word)

Psalm 8: The Splendor of the Night Sky (meditation)

## God's Creation:

Jeremiah 18:1–6: In the Potter's Hands (contemplation)

Job 1:20–21: Prayer of Surrender (prayer word)

Psalm 104: God's Creative Power (meditation)

Psalm 19: A Rose (contemplation)

Job 38–39: The Heart and Mind of Job (meditative reading)

## Spiritual Freedom:

Romans 9:20–21: Letting Go (contemplation)

Exodus 3:1–6: Before the Burning Bush (contemplation)

Genesis 22:1–18: Choice in Freedom (contemplation)

Philippians 3:7–11: Dialogue with Christ (journaling)

Romans 8:18–25: Prayer of Healing (meditation)

Isaiah 45:9–13: Praying Over Our Times (meditation)

Hebrews 11:17–19: Meeting Isaac (meditation)

I Corinthians 9:19–23: The Eyes of Jesus (centering prayer)

Philippians 1:21–26: Descent into Prison (contemplation)

## Commitment:

John 3:22–32: In His Light (centering prayer)

I Samuel 3:1–11: God Speaks My Name (contemplation)

Luke 1:26–38: With Mary (contemplation)

Wisdom 9:1–12: To Speak with Wisdom (journaling)

Romans 8:31–39: Conversation with Jesus (contemplation)

Ephesians 3:14–21: Praying with Paul (meditation)

# Bibliography

1. Anderson, Bernard W. *Understanding the Old Testament.* Englewood Cliffs, NJ: Prentice-Hall, 1975.

2. Barclay, William. *The Daily Study Bible Series.* Philadelphia: Westminster Press, 1975.

3. Barth, Karl. *A Shorter Commentary on Romans.* Richmond: John Knox Press, 1963.

4. Bridges, Robert, ed. *Poems of Gerard Manley Hopkins.* New York: Oxford University Press, 1948.

5. Bright, John. *Jeremiah.* Garden City, NY: Doubleday and Co., 1965.

6. Brown, Raymond E. *The Birth of the Messiah.* Garden City, NY: Image Books, 1979.

7. Brown, Raymond E. *The Gospel according to John I–XII.* Garden City, NY: Doubleday and Co., 1966.

8. Brown, Raymond E., et al. *The Jerome Biblical Commentary.* Englewood Cliffs, NJ: Prentice-Hall, 1968.

9. Caird, G. B. *Saint Luke.* London: Penguin Books, 1963.

10. Cowan, Marian, and John C. Futrell. *The Spiritual Exercises of St. Ignatius of Loyola: A Handbook for Directors*. New York: Le Jacq Publishing, 1982.

11. Dahood, Mitchell. *Psalms I, II, III*. Garden City, NY: Doubleday and Co., 1966, 1968, 1970.

12. de Mello, Anthony. *Sadhana, a Way to God*. St. Louis: Institute of Jesuit Sources, 1978.

13. English, John. *Spiritual Freedom*. Guelph, ON: Loyola House, 1974.

14. Ferrucci, Piero. *What We May Be*. Los Angeles: J. P. Tarcher, 1982.

15. Fitzmeyer, Joseph. *The Gospel according to Luke I–IX*. Garden City, NY: Doubleday and Co., 1981.

16. Fleming, David. *The Spiritual Exercises of St. Ignatius: A Literal Translation and a Contemporary Reading*. St. Louis: Institute of Jesuit Sources, 1978.

17. Heschel, Abraham J. *The Prophets*. New York: Harper and Row, 1962.

18. Jung, Carl G. *Man and His Symbols*. New York: Valor Publications, 1964.

19. Leslie, Elmer A. *The Psalms.* New York: Abingdon Press, 1949.

20. Magaña, José, S.J. *A Strategy for Liberation.* Hicksville, NY: Exposition Press, 1974.

21. Maloney, George A., S.J. *Prayer of the Heart.* Notre Dame, IN: Ave Maria Press, 1981.

22. McKenzie, John. *Second Isaiah.* Garden City, NY: Doubleday and Co., 1968.

23. McKenzie, John. *Dictionary of the Bible.* Milwaukee: Bruce Publishing, 1965.

24. Orr, William, and James Arthur Walther. *I Corinthians.* Garden City, NY: Doubleday and Co., 1976.

25. Pennington, M. Basil. *Centering Prayer.* Garden City, NY: Image Books, 1982.

26. Pope, Marvin H. *Job.* Garden City, NY: Doubleday and Co., 1965.

27. Rahner, Karl. *Spiritual Exercises.* New York: Herder and Herder, 1956.

28. Simons, George F. *Journal for Life, Part One: Foundations.* Chicago: ACTA Publications, 1975.

29. Speiser, E. A. *Genesis*. Garden City, NY: Doubleday and Co., 1964.

30. Thompson, Francis. *The Hound of Heaven*. New York: Dodd, Mead and Co., 1963.

31. Veltri, John, S.J. *Orientations, Vol. I: A Collection of Helps for Prayer*. Guelph, ON: Loyola House, 1979.

32. Veltri, John, S.J. *Orientations, Vol. II: Annotation 19: Tentative Edition*. Guelph, ON: Loyola House, 1981.

# About the Authors

JACQUELINE SYRUP BERGAN, a wife, mother, and grandmother, likes to say that she went from putting people to sleep as a nurse anesthetist to waking them up through her ministry of retreat work and spiritual direction. Jacqueline offers spiritual direction through Sacred Ground Spirituality Center in St. Paul, MN, and Spiritual Directors International. She lives with her husband Leonard and family in Bear Trap Lake, WI

MARIE SCHWAN, CSJ, was a member of the Congregation of St. Joseph. She spent a number of years focused on post-Vatican II and biblical renewal within her community and beyond, including 14 years as associate director of the Jesuit Retreat House in Oshkosh, WI. Marie Schwan passed away on December 30, 2014.

# Also Available

## RETREAT IN THE REAL WORLD

ANDY ALEXANDER, SJ
MAUREEN McCANN WALDON
LARRY GILLICK, SJ

$14.95 • Pb • 2913-8

What do you imagine when someone mentions the word "retreat"? Your mind may conjure images of withdrawing from life and traveling to a distant retreat house away from home. But who has time for that? What if you didn't have to go to a retreat to enjoy its many benefits . . . what if the retreat came to you?

*Retreat in the Real World* offers the unique opportunity to create an in-depth, self-directed Ignatian retreat on your own time. This 34-week retreat can be started at any point in the calendar year and can be experienced anywhere that works for you. You can even experience the retreat by yourself or in conjunction with others.

# Also Available

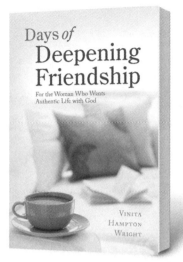

**DAYS OF DEEPENING FRIENDSHIP**

VINITA HAMPTON WRIGHT

$13.95 • PB • 2811-7

Acclaimed author and speaker Vinita Hampton Wright invites women to embark upon a dynamic friendship with God that is both stunning in its wisdom and delightful in its daily unfolding. Using Scripture, meditations, stories, and written exercises, *Days of Deepening Friendship* encourages women to radically rethink their approach to God and to explore the deeper regions of this very special relationship.

Wright taps the proven wisdom of Ignatian spirituality by employing prayer, imagination, action, and reflection, making *Days of Deepening Friendship* an ideal spiritual workshop for women looking to be free to be themselves and to express themselves—without fear—to God.

# Continue your Ignatian spirituality journey online . . .

Learn more about prayer, spiritual direction,
retreats, and how to make good decisions at

# www.ignatianspirituality.com